Brooklands
Books

☆ A BROOKLANDS ☆
'ROAD TEST' LIMITED EDITION

BERKELEY
SPORTSCARS

Compiled by
R.M.Clarke

ISBN 1 85520 4312

BROOKLANDS BOOKS LTD.
P.O. BOX 146, COBHAM,
SURREY, KT11 1LG. UK

Brooklands
Books

ACKNOWLEDGEMENTS

For more than 35 years, Brooklands Books have been publishing compilations of road tests and other articles from the English speaking world's leading motoring magazines. We have already published more than 600 titles, and in these we have made available to motoring enthusiasts some 20,000 stories which would otherwise have become hard to find. For the most part, our books focus on a single model, and as such they have become an invaluable source of information. As Bill Boddy of *Motor Sport* was kind enough to write when reviewing one of our Gold Portfolio volumes, the Brooklands catalogue "must now constitute the most complete historical source of reference available, at least of the more recent makes and models."

Even so, we are constantly being asked to publish new titles on cars which have a narrower appeal than those we have already covered in our main series. The economics of book production make it impossible to cover these subjects in our main series, but Limited Edition volumes like this one give us a way to tackle these less popular but no less worthy subjects. This additional range of books is matched by a Limited Edition - Extra series, which contains volumes with further material to supplement existing titles in our Road Test and Gold Portfolio ranges.

Both the Limited Edition and Limited Edition - Extra series maintain the same high standards of presentation and reproduction set by our established ranges. However, each volume is printed in smaller quantities - which is perhaps the best reason we can think of why you should buy this book now. We would also like to remind readers that we are always open to suggestions for new titles; perhaps your club or interest group would like us to consider a book on your particular subject?

Finally, we are more than pleased to acknowledge that Brooklands Books rely on the help and co-operation of those who publish the magazines where the articles in our books originally appeared. For this present volume, we gratefully acknowledge the continued support of the publishers of *Autocar, Autosport, Berkeley Cars Ltd., Car and Driver, Car Life, Classic Cars, Modern Motor, Motor, Motor Cycle, Motor Cycling, Motor Trend, New Zealand Car, Road & Track, Small Car Guide, Sporting Cars, Sports Car World* and *Wheels* for allowing us to include their valuable and informative copyright stories.

R.M. Clarke.

CONTENTS

THE BERKELEY

A MOULDED MINIATURE

Famous Caravan Manufacturers Introduce an Ingenious Small Sports Car

A NEW approach to the problem of how to build a car is a refreshing surprise, particularly when some of the industry's difficulty in finding ready markets is blamed on lack of foresight and enterprise. Morever, it requires courage to dive headlong into a pond which is showing such alarming signs of drought. Such, however, is the air of enthusiasm and self-confidence at Biggleswade, where the Berkeley Coachwork Company are about to put a new small sports car into limited production that one must share their optimism.

The new project is born of the design artistry of Lawrence Bond (responsible for the three-wheeled Bond Minicar) and the Berkeley Company's skill and experience in the use of glass-reinforced polyester resin, henceforth referred to as G.R.P.R., as a stressed constructional material. For some years past it has been used successfully for the shells of Berkeley touring caravans, and the company's proficiency in its use may be indicated by the fact that the shell of the 14ft Delight needs but two mouldings.

The visitor to Biggleswade is surprised to find such a large factory devoted to the construction of caravans, but less so when he learns that over 25,000 vans have been built there in ten years. Clearly no factory with such a background would lightly undertake the building of a car; in fact an initial production rate of some 50 a week is planned —without affecting caravan production.

This design, which was initiated about five years ago, breaks fresh ground in important respects.

First, it is probably unique in the world in having a composite body and chassis constructed, in three bolted-together sections, of moulded G.R.P.R. True, there are local stiffeners and a bulkhead, fabricated in aluminium sheet and riveted into the main structure, but the G.R.P.R. is subjected to stresses. If seriously damaged, any one of the three basic sections (base, front and rear) may be replaced without affecting the whole. The material used is immensely tough, strong and resistant to impact loads. It has, moreover, the invaluable virtue of being non-corrosive and of being simple to patch locally.

The Berkeley is also the only four-wheeled British car now marketed with front-wheel drive, and the success of certain Continental constructors with f.w.d. should ensure that it will meet with no sales resistance abroad on this score. It is powered by the 322 c.c. two-stroke, twin-cylinder Anzani, a small air-cooled unit in increasing favour with constructors of miniature cars.

This is placed ahead of the front wheel centre-line, and drives through a three-speed-and-reverse Albion gear box (of motor-cycle type) and open chain to a Tufnol "silent" sprocket, bolted direct to the diminutive Bond-designed spur-type differential. This differential is to the left of the chassis centre-line, and the drive shaft to the wheel on that side is somewhat shorter than the other.

A steel sub-frame spreads the weight of engine and gear box over a wide area of the punt-like base, those units being jointly supported on the sub-frame at three points, with two vertical Silentbloc bushes at the front and one horizontal bush beneath the gear box to the rear. Girling telescopic suspension units, each with an enclosed coil spring and hydraulic damper, carry the car at all four corners, but the geometry at front and rear is quite different. Thus there are swinging half-axles at the rear, each a welded tubular member in the shape of a distorted A, of which the two extremities are pivoted on two widely spaced pick-up points along the chassis centre-line. They hinge on Silentbloc rubber bushes.

At the front are wishbones of unequal length, their outer ends knuckle-attached to malleable iron stub-axle housings, with which the steering arms are integrally cast. The inner arms of the lower and longer wishbones pass through slots cut in the raised sides of the punt. The lower ends of the suspension units are attached to the upper wishbones, their upper ends to brackets which extend from the bulkhead structure, and are braced

A neat engine installation gives excellent accessibility. The 322 c.c. two-stroke Anzani is fed from a 3½-gallon gravity fuel tank. With a power output of 15 b.h.p. and a kerb weight of under 5½ cwt, the Berkeley can approach 70 m.p.h. and 60 m.p.g.

by a cross-member above the engine. The free length of these suspension units is, incidentally, very easily adjusted, so that the rig of the car (i.e., its suspension geometry) can be kept more or less constant under differing load conditions.

Brakes are Girling hydraulic. A substantial iron brake drum is used, cast in one with the hub and having five wheel pick-up studs threaded into lugs evenly disposed about its periphery. A pistol-grip hand brake lever is linked by cable to the rear wheel shoes.

The gear lever operates in a quadrant mounted on the steering column to the driver's left. The gear positions are all in one plane, necessitated by the motor cycle-type gear box, the positions (from top to bottom) being reverse, neutral, first, second and third.

The attractive and neatly finished body of the Berkeley carries two adults, who have plenty of leg room and stowage space for odds and ends—a detail about which a caravan manufacturer is naturally conscious. Behind them is a detachable panel; this conceals an additional space moulded in the shape of a small seat and foot well, and large enough for two children aged up to, say, eight years. The spare wheel and tyre is normally carried in this well,

be bettered. The prototype tried had already covered over 4,000 miles of hard testing but seemed none the worse.

A maximum of nearly 70 m.p.h. is claimed, but there was no opportunity to confirm this. The little engine emits a hearty crackle, its two exhausts discharging beneath the car and forward of the drive shafts, with no tail pipe extensions.

On the overrun the engine cuts very cleanly to allow quick upward changes, and, considering the limited cylinder dimensions, acceleration in the two lower gears is quite brisk. The step-up from second to top is wide, and top-gear pick-up is naturally less lively. At low speeds in top gear the Berkeley is notably smooth and tractable. The ride is firm without harshness, but the real joys of the Berkeley are its freedom from roll, and ability to tackle corners at speeds which challenge one's courage and discretion.

Braking power, in terms of both efficiency of the mechanism and tyre adhesion, is quite outstanding, and the steering is light and accurate. The lack of self-centring, synonymous with front-wheel drive and this particular suspension layout, seems strange at first, but is really missed only during a succession of small-radius bends. The prototype gear change

The spare wheel is normally stowed in the rear compartment. There are flashing indicators and two wiper blades, but clock and fuel gauge are extras. Six-inch Wipac head lamps will be fitted

was a little tricky, but the production quadrant is expected to provide better definition.

Certainly the Berkeley promises to be one of the safest small cars on the road, and if an alternative, more powerful version is marketed, as at present projected, it should prove a potent competition car.

Brief Specification

ENGINE

Position		Front, in unit with transmission.
No. of cyls.		2, air-cooled.
Bore and stroke ...		60 x 57 mm (2.36 x 2.24-in).
Displacement		322 c.c. (19.65 cu in).
Valve position ...		Ported two-stroke.
Max. b.h.p.		15 at 4,800 r.p.m.
Carburettor		Single Amal, gravity feed.
Fuel tank capacity ...		3¼ Imp. galls.
Batteries		2 6-volt 12-amp hr.

TRANSMISSION

Clutch		Wet multi-plate.
Speeds: lever position ...		3 forward, 1 reverse. Quadrant, on steering column.
Overall ratios ...		Top 5.27, 2nd 8.43, 1st 13.85, rev. 17.25.
Final drive		Chain.

CHASSIS

Brakes		Girling hydraulic 7 x 1¼-in. Front, 2 L.S. Rear L and T.
Suspension		Front, independent, coil springs and wishbones; rear, independent, coil springs and swing axles.
Steering		Burman worm and nut.
Tyres		Michelin 5.20 x 12.

DIMENSIONS

Wheelbase		5ft 10in.
Track		3ft 8in.
Overall length ...		10ft 3in.
Overall width ...		4ft 2in.
Overall height ...		3ft 5⅜in.
Turning circle ...		28ft.
Kerb weight (with hood)		5¼ cwt.

Sleek lines disguise a wheelbase of only 5ft 10in and 3ft 8in track, and the unbroken under-surface is almost equally smooth. Neat windscreen supports serve also as grab-handles, and large brake drums are integral with the wheel hubs. Michelin 5.20 x 12 tyres are standard

but it can also be stowed on a long, deep shelf beneath the scuttle. A carriage key releases the rear seat backrest, revealing a further luggage locker in the tail.

A production line for the Berkeley has already been prepared. This starts with the preparation of the glass fibre moulds and ends with the finished product, and it is planned that a car will leave the line every 44 minutes. The chemical processes involved are such that production can be stepped up only by creating another complete production line, but the space required is remarkably compact, and this would clearly involve little difficulty. It is hoped to review production methods at Biggleswade when the process has reached a more mature stage of development, and when production is in full swing.

ROAD IMPRESSIONS

ONE settles in the Berkeley driving seat with an intuition that it has a surprise or two in store. There is abundant leg room and width inside, except at shoulder height, where the upper edges of the doors limit movement when two are carried. Shallow, leathercloth-covered cushion and backrest are well shaped; a shorter steering column would allow a longer reach to the wheel. A deep and stoutly mounted curved screen, with particularly neat frame, gives excellent protection and visibility that could scarcely

Lawrence Bond, designer (left), and Charles Panter, managing director, with the second prototype. The base, in glass-reinforced polyester resin with sheet aluminium stiffeners, carries the Anzani engine and transmission at the front. Mounting brackets are ready to receive the rear swing axles

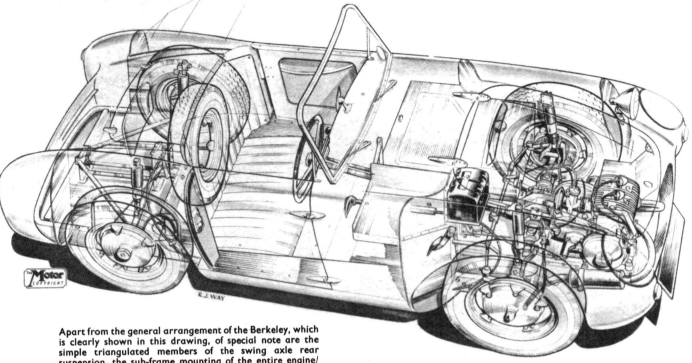

Apart from the general arrangement of the Berkeley, which is clearly shown in this drawing, of special note are the simple triangulated members of the swing axle rear suspension, the sub-frame mounting of the entire engine/transmission assembly and the Girling motorcycle-type suspension units.

The BERK

A New, Ultra-light Two-seater of Unorthodox Design in which Plastics Play a Very Large Part

WHEN in *The Motor* of June 6 this year, "King-pin" put forward a plea for "... a small and relatively gentle roadster ... a fresh-air car that is easy to park and handy in traffic ...", he could scarcely have realized how quickly a vehicle, broadly lining up with his requirements, would become available.

Yesterday, a new car was announced by a new manufacturer, at least so far as cars are concerned. It is the Berkeley, designed by Laurie Bond, originator of the Bond Minicar, and is to be manufactured by the well-known caravan concern—Berkeley (Sales and Export), Ltd., of Biggleswade, Beds. A small, open two-seater with occasional accommodation for a couple of small children, the Berkeley has a claimed top-gear performance in excess of 65 m.p.h., achieved with a twin-cylinder, air-cooled, two-stroke power unit of under 350 c.c. in conjunction with very light weight.

After considerable research into the suitability of glass fibre/polyester resin mouldings for caravan construction, the Berkeley concern were the first to market such a caravan and produce it in considerable quantities. The design of the Berkeley car centres around extensive use of similar plastics mouldings, so the adoption by Berkeley of Bond's design was a commonsense arrangement.

Glass fibre/polyester resin plastics combine considerable strength, both from a ductile and impact point of view, with very light weight, plus the fact that the characteristics can, within limits, be adjusted in the "mix," to suit various requirements. It is these factors, coupled with a relative ease of moulding calling for little highly expensive equipment, that have undoubtedly influenced the designer in his aim to produce a light, economical vehicle to sell at a moderate price and offer an acceptable degree of performance. A further advantage of this particular form of fabrication lies in the fact that metal sections can be joined into the plastics structure as it is moulded.

The main structure of the Berkeley is a stressed-skin body-chassis unit made up of three parts—a pontoon under-section, a nose section and a tail unit. Each is moulded from glass-reinforced plastics and stiffened where necessary by metal sections bonded or riveted to each moulding. Bolted together, the three portions form, in effect, a capsule, rigid in itself within the limits of the plastics material and strengthened at the points of greatest stress or, as in the case

of the area beneath the cockpit, where the tubular form has to be broken into.

The foundation of the vehicle is the under-section—a one-piece, dish-shaped moulding running the full length and width. Two inverted L-shaped light alloy pressings run longitudinally along each edge of the centre portion forming, in conjunction with the dished sides, a box section of considerable strength and

THE BERKELEY CAR

Engine			Chassis details		
Cylinders	...	...	2	Brakes	Girling hydraulic (2 l.s. front)
Bore ...	...	...	60 mm.		
Stroke	...	...	57 mm.	Brake drum diameter	7 in.
Cubic capacity	...	322 c.c.	Friction lining area	65 sq. in.
Piston area ...	...	8.8 sq. in.	Suspension:	
Valves	...	...	Rotary in crankcase	Front	Unequal wishbone i.f.s. with Girling coil spring units
Compression ratio	...	8.5 to 1		
Engine performance			Rear	Swing axle i.r.s., with Girling coil spring units
Max. power ...	...	15 b.h.p.		
at ...	...	...	5,000 r.p.m.	Shock absorbers	Hydraulic, built into Girling spring units
Max. b.m.e.p.	...	63 lb. per sq. in.		
at ...	...	...	3,500 r.p.m.	Wheel type ...	Special lightweight, 5-stud fixing
B.H.P. per sq. in. piston area	...	1.71		
			Tyre size ...	5.20—12
Piston speed at max. power	1,870 ft. per min. at 5,000 r.p.m.	Steering gear ...	Burman worm and nut
Engine details			**Dimensions**		
Carburetter...	...	"Amal" type 376/38	Wheelbase ...	5 ft. 10 in.
Ignition timing control			Track:	
		Fixed	Front ...	3 ft. 8 in.
Plugs: make and type	Champion L.11S, 14 mm.	Rear ...	3 ft. 8 in.
Fuel pump ...	...	Nil	Overall length	10 ft. 3 in.
Fuel capacity	...	3½ gallons	Overall width	4 ft. 2 in.
Oil filter ...	...	Nil	Overall height	41¾ in.
Oil capacity	...	Petroil system	Ground clearance ...	5 in.
Cooling system	...	Air	Turning circle ...	28 ft.
Water capacity	...	Nil	Dry weight ...	5¼ cwt.
Electrical system	...	12-volt coil ignition		
Battery capacity	...	12 amp./hr.	**Performance Factors** (at dry weight)	
Transmission			Piston area, sq. in. per ton ...	32
Clutch ...	...	3-plate		
Gear ratios:			Brake lining area, sq. in. per ton ...	236
Top ...	...	5.27		
2nd ...	...	8.43	Top gear m.p.h. per 1,000 r.p.m.	11.8
1st ...	...	13.85		
Rev. ...	...	17.25	Top gear m.p.h. per 1,000 ft./min. piston speed	34.0
Prop. shaft ...	...	Front wheel drive		
Final drive ...	Roller chain, through diff. and Hardy Spicer half shafts	Litres per ton-mile...	2,980

Motor COPYRIGHT

R. J. WAY

In general appearance and despite its diminutive size, the new car follows closely the lines of many current sports cars.

rigidity. Three further members are set transversely, the two forward ones being of wide box section. Thus, the portion of the base which receives least support from the upper mouldings is well stiffened against longitudinal, transverse and twisting stresses.

The forward portion of the pontoon carries the engine, gearbox and transmission (the Berkeley is driven at the front wheels), which are mounted on a substantial steel sub-frame that, linking up with the forward aluminium cross member, also serves to stiffen the front. At the rear, a box-shaped aluminium section

...ELEY Car

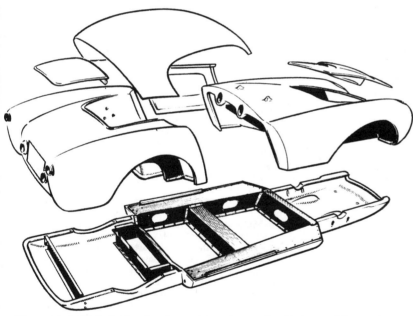

The stressed-skin body/chassis unit comprises three main plastics mouldings, reinforced where necessary with moulded-in aluminium sections. Also shown is the detachable hardtop, an optional extra which is also made of glass fibre/polyester resin. The light alloy stiffening members are shown shaded.

behind the rear main cross member combines with yet another aluminium pressing right at the back to give rear end rigidity and provide supports for the centre pivot of the swing-axle rear suspension.

The upper nose moulding, likewise, is rendered even more rigid by a four-sided aluminium "box" which forms the sides and rearward end of the engine compartment and by a shelf upon which are mounted the auxiliaries and the 3½-gallon fuel tank. In the more lightly stressed tail moulding, sufficient rigidity is imparted by a plastics bulkhead which forms the forward end

of the luggage boot and the sides and base of the spare wheel compartment; only the inner sides of the wings are of metal.

Such, then, is the basic structure of this new and interesting vehicle.

The power unit is the air-cooled 322 c.c. British Anzani two-stroke twin, and in the case of that installed in the Berkeley it has an output of 15 b.h.p. at 5,000 r.p.m. (a top gear speed of 59 m.p.h.). Set well forward, close to the wide, slightly underhung air intake, the engine is cooled by ducts which direct the incoming air directly on to the cylinders and cylinder head, whence it is dispersed through apertures beneath the front wings and by a rearward slot in the alligator panel at the top of the nose. Fuel is gravity fed to an Amal Type 376/38 carburetter and each cylinder exhausts through a separate pipe and silencer. Ignition is by twin coils, one to each sparking plug, the 12-volt electrical system being supplied from a Siba Dynastarter driving and driven directly off the crankshaft. Lubrication is by the petroil system.

A dry, multi-plate clutch, driven by a roller chain from the engine, transmits the drive to an Albion motorcycle pattern gearbox having three forward speeds and reverse, selection being of the non-positive-stop variety effected through a simple linkage by a steering-column gearshift. The entire engine/gearbox unit is mounted at three points on the forward sub-frame previously referred to, with rubber inserts to damp out any low-speed engine vibration.

Drive to the differential, which is mounted close up behind the gearbox on a three-bolt rocking mounting to allow for chain adjustment, is by a further roller chain driving over a Tufnol sprocket to reduce whine. The substantial half-shafts which connect to the front wheels have Hardy-Spicer universal joints at each end.

The independently suspended front hubs, mounted on malleable swivel castings with integral track-rod arms, are carried on unequal length wishbones pivoting on Silentbloc bushes and give a roll centre of 4½ inches above the ground. They operate in conjunction with single coil springs surrounding Girling suspension units incorporating coil springs and dampers. The lower wishbones are attached to the side members of the engine sub-frame while those at the top couple to a steel transverse member attached to the metal side of the engine compartment with bracing stays to give extra strength.

The front wheels are linked by a three-piece track rod actuated through a Burman worm and nut steering gear calling for 2½ turns of the steering wheel from one lock to the other.

Two large, triangulated tubular members provide the swing axle independent suspension at the rear. They, too, operate with Girling suspension units and pivot on Silentbloc bushes attached to a pair of steel brackets located, horizontally, by a steel bar linking the two rearmost transverse stiffening members and,

In the photograph above, the moulded-in facia is seen in its most fully equipped form. The steering column gearshift, operating in a quadrant, is handy and practical. Also discernible is the under-scuttle parcel tray. Below is the spare wheel compartment which can also be used as an occasional seat with the wheel carried elsewhere. The light coloured panel in the back gives access to yet another locker.

vertically, by having their feet bonded into the plastics base of the car.

At both front and rear, the brakes are Girling hydraulic, working in 7-in. ribbed drums, those at the front having two leading shoes. A total brake lining area of no less than 65 sq. in. to deal with an unladen dry weight of only 5½ cwt. suggests exceptional life between brake adjustments. The handbrake lever, which is of the umbrella-handle variety, operates on the rear wheels only, connection being by Bowden cable. The pressed steel wheel rims, with 5.20-12 Michelin tyres have five flanges which bolt up to lugs cast on to the brake drums.

In a vehicle of such unusual integral construction, it is not, perhaps, strictly correct to speak of "bodywork" but, for want of a better word, we will keep the familiar term in describing the enveloping mass which accommodates passengers and luggage.

Despite the fact that the Berkeley is but 10 ft. 3 in. long and 4 ft. 2 in. wide, it is, proportionally, a true miniature motorcar with the pleasant lines one associates with the better examples of British and Continental sports-car coachwork of current design. Indeed, photographically, it is not until one views it in relation to its occupants as in a photograph on this page, that the Berkeley's very modest dimensions really become apparent.

The BERKELEY Car

Nevertheless, the cockpit provides surprisingly generous accommodation for two average-sized people and leg room which suggests that a six-footer may find himself less cramped than in some larger vehicles.

In the interests of weight saving and keeping down the cost, the bench-type seat is not adjustable; it is equipped with plastics upholstery over an interior-spring cushion.

The driver sits behind a deep, curved windscreen of toughened glass equipped with twin-arm electrically operated screen-wipers. The 16-in. diameter steering wheel is of the two-spoke variety and is plastics covered. On the right, below the scuttle, is the umbrella grip of the handbrake and, ahead, the neat if rather sparsely equipped facia panel which is moulded in one with the main nose section. Behind it and below is the deep parcel shelf-cum-stiffening-member; this runs the full width of the car. The two doors, each of which is a plastics moulding with wooden capping, have strap-operated inside catches and large pockets.

Behind the seat squab, a hinged panel on the top of the tail gives access to a compartment which normally carries the spare wheel and some luggage. The base of this compartment is so shaped that, with the top panel removed, for which purpose it has special hinges, the spare wheel can be transferred to the parcel shelf where there is plenty of room for it. When this is done, occasional seating is available for one or two small children on short journeys such as being taken to school. Behind the spare-wheel compartment, accessible through another detachable panel, is a further tail locker for more luggage.

Although the model shown to *The Motor* had not yet been fitted with its all-weather equipment, this will be included in the standard specification and consists of a hood which covers both the cockpit and spare-wheel compartment, plus a pair of side curtains. A detachable hardtop will also be available as an optional extra.

Lighting equipment consists of a pair of combined head and side lights recessed into the top of the front wings (the only available point at which they are high enough off the road to comply with the law), rear and stop lights, and flashing indicator lamps operated by a switch which incorporates a warning light and is mounted on the scuttle by the driver's right hand.

A short run in one of the production prototypes suggested that the Berkeley is a "real" car in more than just appearance. Once one became accustomed to somewhat pronounced oversteer and a taxi-like steering lock, corners could safely be taken with considerable enterprise. Acceleration and top speed, despite the diminutive engine, were sufficient to give many other motorists a rapidly diminishing rear-end view of this unorthodox little vehicle. On the other hand one could potter quietly through traffic at a docile 15 m.p.h. in top gear or cruise placidly along open roads at 35-40 m.p.h.

The retail price of the Berkeley in standard form is expected to be in the region of £575 inclusive of purchase tax, which figure should attract a sufficient section of the car-buying public that upholds "King-pin's" plea to justify the courage both of the designer and the manufacturers. Although only a few individually assembled models have yet been built, a production line is well on the way to completion alongside those of the caravans upon which the Berkeley name has been built, and which will continue to be made. An output of 50 Berkeley cars per week is planned once assembly gets into its full stride, and first production models are expected to be in the hands of distributors during the first week in October.

OPTIONAL EXTRAS

Detachable plastics hard-top; tonneau cover; luggage grid; badge bar; electric clock; fuel contents guage.

Two adults and two small children is the maximum capacity of the Berkeley. The true proportions of the car in relation to average sized adults are indicated in this illustration.

Britain's Mini-Sports Car THE BERKELEY

True size of the Berkeley is shown in this photo —unless the young lady is over 6 feet tall.

The tiny air-cooled engine is surrounded by a box which acts as an air duct.

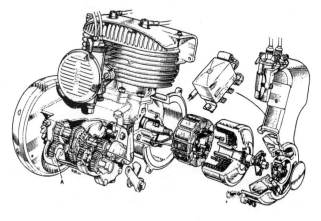

BY PETER D. SHERIDAN-YOUNG

DESIGNED BY LAURIE BOND, originator of the Bond 3-wheeler mini-car, the new Berkeley ultra-light sports car is now in production with a target of fifty a week by the end of 1956 and a price tag of $1100 f.o.b. England.

The manufacturer is Berkeley Coachwork Ltd., who normally make caravans (trailer homes). Their car, a small, open two-seater with space for two small children, is designed to utilize fiberglass throughout even in the unique underbody structure. This is, however, reinforced with some sheet aluminum, bonded and riveted where necessary.

Stirling Moss himself drove the car around the Goodwood circuit for its TV debut and was amazed at its outstanding performance and top speed which approaches 70 mph.

The powerplant is a British Anzani two-stroke rotary-valve twin which develops 15 bhp from 322 cc. There are three forward speeds and a reverse, and the vehicle has front wheel drive with independent suspension on all four wheels .

The bodywork is not painted, but is available with self-coloring in red, pale blue, green, and black. The surface finish is first class, much better than most U.S. fiberglass bodies I have seen. Styling and proportions are very well done, as shown in the photographs. The one item not scaled down is the passenger space and leg room which is excellent by any sports car standards.

The weight is an unbelievable 616 lbs., and this accounts for the performance—on the order of 0-50 mph in 20 seconds. Other powerplants up to 750 cc are, however, to be made available ●

THE Berkeley is an entirely new kind of car. Designed by Laurie Bond, the originator of the Minicar, it bristles with novel features. For a start, it is the smallest and lightest four-wheeled car on the market. Yet it has a delightfully modern appearance and, above all, it is definitely a sports car.

Berkeley Coachwork, Ltd., of Biggleswade, Beds., who manufacture the little machine, are pioneers in plastic caravan construction. It is thus no surprise that the body is of glass fibre/polyester resin. What is entirely novel, however, is the

JOHN BOLSTER TRIES

The BERKELEY

An entirely new "baby" sports-car—70 m.p.h. and over 50 m.p.g., with outstanding road holding and braking—for under £600

employment of this kind of body as a chassis frame. In effect, there are two large-diameter main tubular members, of which half the tube is plastic and the other half aluminium, bonded and riveted together. There are also aluminium cross members, and a sheet aluminium box reinforces the engine compartment.

The suspension is independent all round. The front wheels, which are driven, are on unequal length wishbones, and are steered by a three-piece track rod from a Burman box. The half-shafts are of Hardy Spicer manufacture, with two universal joints apiece and sliding splines. The rear wheels are on tubular triangulated swing axles. The suspension medium is by Girling, in the form of helical springs and telescopic dampers. The hydraulic brakes are also of Girling manufacture, with 7 ins. drums and two leading shoes in front. The wheels are in the form of rims, bolting on to lugs on the drums, and are fitted with 5.20 x 12 ins. Michelin tyres.

The engine is an Anzani vertical twin two-stroke, specially tuned for sports performance. It has ducted air cooling, and in addition to piston controlled ports it has a rotary inlet valve. The bore and stroke are 60 mm. x 57 mm., giving a capacity of 322 c.c. This may seem very small, but over 15 b.h.p. is developed at 5,000 r.p.m., and the low

ROOMY, in spite of its diminutive size, the car can accommodate two children in the space behind the seats. The wheels are merely detachable rims, Renault fashion.

speed torque is excellent. Thus, it is amply big enough to give a spirited performance in a car that only weighs 5½ cwt.

A chain in an oil-bath case takes the drive to the three-plate clutch, and the three-speed gearbox gives overall ratios of 5.27, 8.43, and 13.85 to 1. The final chain obtains some oil mist from a breather, and drives the spur-type differential through a Tufnol sprocket, which gives silent running and increased chain life. The engine and gearbox are carried ahead of the half-shafts, and are mounted on rubber to avoid transmission of vibration and noise. A 12-volt Siba dynastarter is coupled direct to the crankshaft.

When I entered the car through one of the full-sized doors, I found that the non-adjustable seat gave me plenty of room. The gear lever works on a quadrant under the steering wheel, and would no doubt call for a little practice from those unaccustomed to a progressive change. Personally, I was soon at home with it, the positions, starting at the top, being Reverse, Neutral, 1, 2, 3. One needs to rev. the engine considerably before engaging the clutch, because the flywheel is light and so stalling is possible. Once on the move, one accelerates rapidly up to 20 m.p.h. or so, when second speed may be engaged. This gear is good for over 40 m.p.h. before top goes in.

During hard acceleration, the exhaust note from the twin silencers is fairly healthy, but at the cruising speed of 55 m.p.h. the car is surprisingly quiet. I did not have an opportunity to obtain a timed maximum speed over a measured distance, but it is claimed to be better than 70 m.p.h. without the large screen. Fully equipped, the car proved capable of exceeding 60 m.p.h. on quite short straights. This is magnificent going for 322 c.c., and underlines the efficiency of the streamlining.

The little machine holds the road like a racing car, and has very high cornering power. It behaves like the best Continental F.W.D. cars, and can really be thrown about. Nothing untoward occurs if one lifts one's foot in the middle of a bend, and it is literally im-

SHAPELY rear view of the well-finished glass-fibre/plastic body is reminiscent of the A.C. Ace, but the relatively enormous number plate shows that it is very much smaller!

possible to feel from the steering that this is a *traction*. The handling characteristic is virtually neutral, with just a fraction of understeer to give stability. The steering of the test car was light and very high-geared. Personally, I found it ideal, but some drivers tended to over-steer the car, and so the production version is fractionally less "quick".

The brakes are almost beyond belief. Those who have watched 500 c.c. racing know that a very light vehicle may be slowed down for a corner in an apparently impossibly short distance. The Berkeley behaves just like a racing 500 in this respect, and the roadholding and braking would do credit to a car capable of twice the speed. One seems able to pass almost any car on a winding road, and it is only up long hills that one is conscious of having such a small engine. The ride is fairly hard, but not objectionably so.

The two-stroke engine is very flexible, no doubt because of its rotary valve. It is possible to potter along at a steady 10 m.p.h. in top gear, and to accelerate cleanly from that speed. Naturally, no real performance is available if the gears are not used intelligently, but the car is

perfectly suitable for the slow driver or the beginner.

Behind the seat is a compartment in which the spare wheel is normally carried, but it may be removed and attached to the shelf under the scuttle, where it is out of the passenger's way. The rear compartment can then be occupied by a child, and behind it there is a further space which is used to carry the hood sticks and fabric.

The Berkeley is essentially a practical vehicle, and it is equipped like a full-sized car. It has powerful lights and an electric starter, which acts as a dynamo delivering 90 watts continuously, with a maximum output of 120 watts. Naturally, only time can prove whether there are any snags, but it feels a safe and solidly constructed car, and its phenomenal brakes are potential life-savers. Driven flat out, it never does less than 50 m.p.g., with 60 m.p.g. to reward the more normal driver. At a price in the region of £575, including tax, the Berkeley will be the cheapest sports car on the market as well as the smallest, with a wheelbase of 5 ft. 10 ins., a track of 3 ft. 8 ins., and an overall length of 10 ft. 3 ins. A larger-engined version may later be available.

FLYWEIGHT sports car, scaling only 5¼ cwt., the Berkeley, complete with Stirling Moss, can easily be lifted bodily by four men.

★

COCKPIT (left) is uncomplex in layout. The gearchange is operated by a simple quadrant on the steering column.

Brief Specification

Engine: Anzani two cylinders, air-cooled, 60 mm. x 57 mm. (322 c.c.), two-stroke. Amal gravity-feed carburetter; 15 b.h.p. at 4,800 r.p.m. Mounted in front, in unit with transmission.

Transmission: Wet, three-plate clutch. Three-speed gearbox with reverse; ratios, 5.27, 8.43 and 13.85 to 1; final drive by chain to front wheels.

Body and Frame: Combined structure of resin-bonded glass fibre panelling, aluminium bulkheads and cross members. Independent front suspension by unequal length wishbones and helical springs; independent rear suspension by tubular triangulated swing axles and helical springs. Girling hydraulic brakes, 2LS in front; drums 7 ins. x 1¼ ins. Burman worm and nut steering; 5.20 x 12 ins. tyres on bolt-on wheels.

Equipment: 12-volt lighting and starting (Siba dynastarter).

Dimensions: Wheelbase, 5 ft. 10 ins.; track, 3 ft. 8 ins.; length, 10 ft. 3 ins.; width, 4 ft. 2 ins.; height, 3 ft. 5¾ ins.; weight (kerb), 5¼ cwt.; turning circle, 28 ft.

Make: Berkeley   **Type:** Sports Two-seater

Makers: Berkeley Coachwork (Sales and Export) Ltd., Biggleswade, Bedfordshire

Test Data

CONDITIONS: *Weather: Mild, damp weather, with strong wind blowing down course. (Temperature 55°-58° F., Barometer 29.6 in. Hg.). Surface: Intermittently damp tarmac. Fuel: Premium grade pump fuel (approx. 95 Research Method Octane Rating) with addition of ½ pint S.A.E.30 oil per gallon. Tested with hood and sidescreens erected.*

INSTRUMENTS

Speedometer at 30 m.p.h. ...	...	1½% fast
Distance recorder	...	1½% fast

WEIGHT

Kerb weight (unladen, but with oil and fuel for approx. 50 miles) ...	6½ cwt.
Front/rear distribution of kerb weight	62/38
Weight laden as tested	10 cwt.

MAXIMUM SPEEDS

Flying Quarter Mile

Mean of four opposite runs ...	62.1 m.p.h.
Best one-way time equals ...	65.5 m.p.h.

"Maximile" Speed. (Timed quarter mile after one mile accelerating from rest)

Mean of two opposite runs ...	61.6 m.p.h.
Best one-way time equals ...	63.9 m.p.h.

Speed in gears

Max. speed in 2nd gear	41 m.p.h.
Max. speed in 1st gear	25 m.p.h.

PETROL CONSUMPTION

73.5 m.p.g. at constant 30 m.p.h. on level (oil consumption, 1,180 m.p.g.).

71.0 m.p.g. at constant 40 m.p.h. on level (oil consumption, 1,135 m.p.g.).

55.0 m.p.g. at constant 50 m.p.h. on level (oil consumption 880 m.p.g.).

Overall Petrol Consumption for 911 miles, 19.1 gallons, equals 47.7 m.p.g. (5.9 litres/100 km.).

Touring Fuel Consumption (m.p.g. at steady speed midway between 30 m.p.h. and maximum, less 5% allowance for acceleration) 58.3 m.p.g.

Fuel Tank Capacity (maker's figure) including reserve 3½ gallons

ACCELERATION TIMES from standstill

0-30 m.p.h. ...	...	...	...	10.3 sec.
0-40 m.p.h. ...	...	...	...	16.1 sec.
0-50 m.p.h. ...	...	...	...	30.6 sec.
Standing quarter mile	...	...		28.2 sec.

ACCELERATION TIMES on Upper Ratios

	Top gear	2nd gear
10-30 m.p.h.	22.7 sec.	11.1 sec.
20-40 m.p.h.	20.2 sec.	11.0 sec.
30-50 m.p.h.	23.0 sec.	—

STEERING

Turning circle between kerbs:

Left...	...	...	...	26½ feet
Right	...	...	...	29 feet
Turns of steering wheel from lock to lock				2¼

BRAKES from 30 m.p.h.

1.00g retardation (equivalent to 30 ft. stopping distance) with 50 lb. pedal pressure

0.70g retardation (equivalent to 43 ft. stopping distance) with 25 lb. pedal pressure

HILL CLIMBING at sustained steady speeds.

Max. gradient on top gear   1 in 15.4 (Tapley 145 lb./ton)

Max. gradient on 2nd gear   1 in 8.9 (Tapley 250 lb./ton)

TRACK: FRONT / BACK 3'-8"

OVERALL WIDTH 4'-2"

3'-7½"

GROUND CLEARANCE 5"

SCALE 1:50   5'-8⅜"   **BERKELEY**

10'-2½"

SCREEN FRAME TO FLOOR 34½"   SEAT TO HOOD 38"

12"   8¾"   22¼"   36"   28½"   16¼"   27"   21"   43½"   16"   5½"   39"   19"   24"

DOOR WIDTH   **NOT TO SCALE**

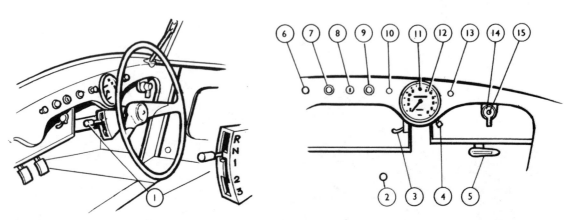

1, Gear lever. 2, Headlamp dip button. 3, Choke control. 4, Trip distance re-setting knob. 5, Handbrake. 6, Lights switch. 7, Horn button. 8, Ignition switch. 9, Starter button. 10, Panel light switch. 11, Dynamo charge warning light. 12, Speedometer and distance recorder. 13, Screen wiper control. 14, Direction indicator switch, and, 15, Warning light.

The Berkeley Sports Two-Seater

Small but roadworthy, the Berkeley adds good looks and finish to a very sporting character.

Excelsior 328 c.c. Engine and a Light, Reinforced Plastics Structure Provide Miniature Sports-Car Performance

IN the boom period for miniature cars which began some months ago, and has received a further boost from petrol rationing, it is perhaps natural that the tiny two-seater Berkeley should be placed at first glance in the same category as the rest. The formula is the same; a small two-stroke, air-cooled engine in a very light chassis; and there is no doubt that with suitably light-footed driving it can be extremely economical of fuel. But there, more or less, the resemblance ends.

The majority of miniature cars have limits of performance which make them predominantly suitable as local run-abouts, possibly as additions to a family stable already containing a full-sized car, but with the Berkeley's diminutive 328 c.c. come a mean maximum speed of over 60 m.p.h. and an apparently tireless capacity for cruising at very little short of this under normal conditions. It thus becomes an entirely practical proposition as an only car, for the man with sporting inclinations but modest means and modest demands for carrying capacity.

Sensibly, in view of the car's purpose, dimensions have been kept to just about the minimum tolerable by human frames travelling long distances. That is to say, a six-foot man of average proportions can sit in it with his legs not straight, but not impossibly bent, and his hair just touching the folding hood, although to lean forward or back would bring his head in contact with the hood frames. Two such men can sit side by side with adequate room for their hips, but freedom for the driver's shoulders is only possible if the passenger sits a little sideways. This particular dimension could be increased by several inches if the tops of the doors, which curve inwards at shoulder height, were cut away to some extent, an improvement which might well tip the scales with many buyers.

The fact is that the majority of men, and certainly the majority of their wives, do not measure up physically to this scale, and will find nothing to complain of in the space provided. The single-piece seat is not adjustable in the normal sense. Both seat and squab being constructed of a thin layer of upholstery upon stretched rubber straps, can however be altered to accommodate individual shapes by tightening or slackening the rubber. The design of the integral body structure, of plastics with light-alloy reinforcement, entails wide boxed side-members in the part occupied by passengers, so that foot- and seat-wells are rather narrow, and tightening the rubber bands helps to avoid a hard edge to the seat for a heavy person. Photographs accompanying this report provide all the evidence necessary that the Berkeley is very low, a feature which has a favourable effect on performance and road holding; entering the car, especially with the hood up and more especially with one passenger already installed, is a fairly acrobatic performance, but although the seats may sometimes be below pavement level the sills are generally high enough for the doors to be opened without obstruction.

Except for low side windows, visibility is excellent even with the hood raised. The external mounting for the headlamps is standard in the United States, but optional in Britain. Wheels consist of detachable rims bolted to the brake drums.

Alternative uses—child or luggage—for the aperture behind the seats. In the former case the spare wheel is transferred to a shelf under the facia (arrowed). An opening panel in the rear (*extreme left*) reveals a stowage in the tail for hood and sidescreens.

The Berkeley Sports Two-Seater

The hood is a little cumbersome to erect, with a two-piece frame which is completely detachable for stowage in the rear, but in conjunction with sidescreens it makes the car completely weatherproof, and not a drop of even heavy rain found its way to the interior. Draughts of some kind are practically inseparable from an open car, and for the few who are troubled by them the most troublesome in the Berkeley occur between the hood and top of the windscreen. On the whole it is snug enough for the kind of owner who does not yet look for such comforts as an interior heater, a difficult item to arrange with a small, front-mounted engine, depending for its cooling upon natural circulation of air.

After an initial production run with a comparable engine of another make, the Berkeley is now issued with an enlarged version of the two-cylinder Excelsior Talisman, a two-stroke unit with petroil lubrication which is mounted well forward of the driven front wheels, and which behaves with model virtue. Whether hot or cold (when the choke is needed almost momentarily), it is started with ease and absolute silence by a 90-watt Siba Dynastart, and rapidly reaches a temperature at which its full 18 b.h.p. can be developed. The torque, moreover, is even and good at all speeds above about 25 m.p.h. in top gear, and it can be driven more slowly than this without jerkiness provided the engine is kept pulling. A two-stroke twin is, of course, the equivalent in its rate of power impulse to a four-cylinder four-stroke,

which together with the extremely light weight makes the Berkeley very flexible by miniature-car standards. The uneven firing on over-run, on the other hand, is a nuisance that has been only partly overcome by very springy rubber engine mountings—one of which failed during our test but has now been altered on production cars—and the same lumpiness is trying with the car at rest.

Sporting Habits

The Berkeley, however, is unlikely to spend much of its time at rest, or in pottering at 20 m.p.h. in top gear. In spite of a performance which cannot now be reckoned as sporting, particularly with two passengers added to its very low weight, it is, in scaled-down fashion, very much a sports car. The 70 m.p.h. which it touched on a downhill stretch in a strong following wind raised no protest from an engine turning at almost 6,000 r.p.m., and a comfortable 5,500 r.p.m. allows 40 m.p.h. to be reached in the second of three gears. Exhaust noise, as with most small two-strokes, is considerable when the engine is pulling, and its volume rises in proportion to the speed, so that prolonged fast cruising becomes something of a mental strain. In common with an earlier design by Laurie Bond, the car has the outlet of a very brief exhaust system ahead of the scuttle (in this case, below the engine undertray), where the noise is more readily transmitted to the occupants, together with some fumes if the hood is closed.

Considered in the context of a sports car in the older, more spartan tradition, the exhaust note would not be thought excessively loud, although it is penetrating, and the engine has the merit of being instantaneously responsive to the accelerator. A motorcycle type of three-speed gearbox, fitted with reverse, connects it to the front-wheel differential, gears being selected by a quadrant lever on the steering column. Rigid and positive in action, this is further improved by a gate mechanism in the quadrant, similar to that found on the tank of a pre-war, hand-change, motorcycle, which ensures positive selection of the right gear. The clutch is mechanically operated, light but inclined to be harsh.

It is in the qualities of suspension and steering that the Berkeley most fully earns the title of sports car, two matters in which it is most affected by the employment, unique in a British four-wheeler, of front-wheel drive. Once only since the war has that system been used here, and with low power and light weight it is resoundingly successful. Girling suspension units, which combine a coil spring and telescopic damper, are fitted to independently-sprung wheels mounted on wishbones at the front and swing-axles at the rear. The moulded "chassis" appears torsionally very stiff (it is completely free from scuttle-shake) and the suspension geometry accurately worked out. As a result, the road-holding would do credit to heavier and more powerful vehicles, making the Berkeley very nearly foolproof at all speeds of which it is capable.

It is, in fact, very difficult to make the wheels slide on any but the most slippery of roads. In contrast to the majority of rear-drive cars, the normal tendency is to quite pronounced oversteer with the car decelerating, which can be converted to understeer by opening the throttle. In other words, it is not only possible, but desirable for stability to accelerate round a corner, and in these conditions a sharper corner or a more slippery road only accentuates the understeer, without causing a sudden break-away. With such a low centre of gravity, roll is negligible, yet in spite of a kerb weight of only 6½ cwt., riding comfort is excellent even over really bad surfaces; limited ground clearance has to be borne in mind nevertheless. The ultimate resistance to abuse by a chassis

Forward mounting of the engine brings into view the plugs, coils, petrol tap and reserve control, brake fluid reservoir and almost all other items needing attention. The battery is inside the car.

2ND copy rec,
& returned Sat.
14-2-04. (61-01 to
me P/M. 13-2-04)
✓ returned 2nd Class 20p

Wed Chevel S de
1036

MR Pallason
Fife, Scotland
01592 774251
Paper 700 x 30
crowleshead lyres
My advertisement Charge
For 12.55 1/4

Rubber straps are adjustable for tension in both seats and squabs.

The Berkeley Sports Two-Seater

The raised headlamps which are a standard fitting for the United States, and optional (instead of lamps flush with the wing) in this country, throw a wide rather than penetrating beam, adequate up to about 55 m.p.h., and may somewhat reduce the all-out speed.

Simplicity of design can, and in the case of the Berkeley does, bring an additional reward in simplicity of maintenance, a point especially interesting to the kind of owner to which it will most appeal. Engine and gearbox are laid bare when the bonnet is opened, with sparking plugs in the forefront, and gravity feed fuel tank and reserve tap easily reached. Raising the tank an inch, and perhaps tilting it slightly forwards, would make sure that the whole reserve supply was effective; at the moment a small quantity is inevitably

left in the tank on a flat or uphill road.

The 12-volt battery is placed inside the car, to the left of the passenger's foot-well where it causes little obstruction. Above it is a large shelf which is left without a lip so that the spare wheel can be carried there if extra luggage or a very small child are to be fitted into the space behind the seats. Behind this again, the hollow tail of the car provides a stowage large enough for the hood, its frame irons, the tonneau cover and the wheel jack. A deep separate shelf ahead of the driver and pockets in both doors completes the carrying space.

Such intelligent planning is important, to give the Berkeley its maximum usefulness. In a world where few people can afford two cars, but many prefer fresh air and fun as part of their money's worth, it should find a wide market.

structure constructed of unorthodox materials is something which cannot be determined in a test of only a thousand miles or so. No undue rattles appeared, but the passenger's door became increasingly difficult to open and shut.

A well-placed small steering wheel controls very light and positive steering, with less than the usual amount of self-centring action. To maintain its very pleasant character it is advisable to lubricate the steering and suspension joints at least as often as the recommended 1,000-mile intervals. A little jerkiness in the transmission is noticeable at the extremes of a lock which allows a turning circle of 26½ feet in one direction, 29 feet in the other.

Braking performance on the test car was excellent on paper, with 100% effectiveness for only 50 lb. pedal pressure, but slightly disappointing in practice owing to ovality in the drums which caused severe judder at some speeds. Brake heating troubles should be unknown, with more than generous lining area in drums which are completely exposed to the air, the wheels being no more than rims bolted to the outside of the drums. A pull-out type of handbrake is fitted.

The Berkeley is very low, as this picture shows.

Specification

Engine

Cylinders	2 (air-cooled)
Bore	58 mm.
Stroke	62 mm.
Cubic capacity	328 c.c.
Piston area	8.2 sq. in.
Valves	None, two-stroke
Compression ratio	7.4/1
Carburetter	Amal
Fuel pump	Gravity feed
Ignition timing control	Automatic
Oil filter	None, petroil lubrication
Max. power (gross)	18 b.h.p.
at	5,000 r.p.m.
Piston speed at max. b.h.p.	2,040 ft./min.

Transmission

Clutch	Albion multi-plate
Top gear	5.27
2nd gear	8.43
1st gear	13.85
Reverse	17.25
Propeller shaft	None, front-wheel drive
Final drive	Open chain
Top gear m.p.h. at 1,000 r.p.m.	11.8
Top gear m.p.h. at 1,000 ft./min. piston speed	34

Chassis

Brakes	Girling hydraulic
Brake drum internal diameter	7 in.
Friction lining area	65 sq. in.
Suspension:	
Front	Wishbones with Girling coil spring and damper units
Rear	Swing-axles with Girling coil spring and damper units
Steering gear	Burman worm and nut
Tyres	5.20—12 tubed

Coachwork and Equipment

Starting handle	No
Battery mounting	Inside cockpit, beside passenger's footwell
Jack	Lever type
Jacking points under chassis, 2 front, 1 rear	
Standard tool kit: Screwdriver, plug spanner, tommy bar, box spanner, 2 open-ended spanners, C-spanner, coach-key for boot, tool roll.	
Exterior lights: 2 head/side, 2 tail, 4 indicator	
Number of electrical fuses	None
Direction indicators	Amber flashing, non self-cancelling
Windscreen wipers	Electric, non self-parking
Windscreen washers	None
Sun vizors	None
Instruments: Speedometer with decimal trip distance recorder.	
Warning lights: Dynamo charge, indicators.	

Locks:	
With ignition key	Ignition
With other key	Bonnet
Glove lockers	None
Map pockets	Two in doors
Parcel shelves: Two under facia, one on rear deck when child's seat unoccupied.	
Ashtrays	None
Cigar lighters	None
Interior lights	Panel light
Interior heater	None
Car radio	None
Extras available: Tonneau cover, clock, ammeter, petrol gauge, over-riders, luggage grid.	
Upholstery material	Vynide
Floor covering	Rubber
Exterior colours standardized	Three
Alternative body styles	None

Maintenance

Lubrication: Petroil mixture, ½ pt. S.A.E.30 oil (reducing to 1/20th gal.) per gallon of petrol.	
Gearbox	½ pint, S.A.E.40
Steering gear lubricant	S.A.E.40
Chassis lubrication	By grease gun every 1,000 miles to 14 points
Ignition timing	7/32 in. on piston b.t.d.c.
Contact-breaker gap	0.025 in.
Sparking plug gap	0.018 in.
Sparking plugs	KLG FE70D

Front wheel toe-in	Nil
Camber angle	2½°
Castor angle	Nil
Steering swivel pin inclination	6°
Tyre pressures:	
Front	14 lb.
Rear	12 lb.
Brake fluid	Girling crimson
Battery type and capacity	12-volt, 23 amp. hr.

The lines are delightfully balanced, and the 12in wheels give the car a better appearance than that of most cars of similar size

BERKELEY SPORTS
TWO-SEATER

HIGH cost and shortage of petrol has brought into prominence the ultra-small economy car. Most of these have proved themselves capable of covering a remarkable number of miles on a gallon of fuel—"fuel" rather than straight petrol, as the popular power unit is the single- or twin-cylinder two-stroke, which uses a mixture of petrol and oil. Originally, owners of these cars had to suffer many shortcomings, usually in the amount of noise, unevenness of ride, poor standard of weather protection, and poor action of and response to a number of the controls.

In countries in which taxation and running costs are even higher than in the United Kingdom, the degree of refinement of these very small cars was greatly improved, but the recent introduction to actual production of the Berkeley sports car has marked a further development still, for this car really does have sporting characteristics, while being also a satisfactory means of economy transport for two people.

Although the model made an impressive public appearance at last October's London Show, it is only recently that the teething troubles have been sorted out, and that the original design has been modified to meet the special requirements of foreign markets as well as of home buyers. During the development period modification has also been made to the twin-cylinder 328 c.c. Excelsior engine, which is now the standard unit, so that the power output is increased.

Thus, in production form, a very small, light car is available with a mean top speed of 65 m.p.h., allied to a good ride, quick response to the controls, and road holding which has yet to be beaten by any competitors in the field of very small cars.

Owing to the extremely light weight (only 6¼ cwt) and the probability of the car being driven frequently with the driver as sole occupant, it was decided to alter the Road Test policy on this occasion and take the acceleration figures without the usual accompanying passenger. As the speedo-meter needle moved steadily, it was possible to calibrate it against the electrical instrument normally carried, and thus the driver was able to take accurate figures single-handed.

The customary weight of driver, passenger and test equipment is about 3 cwt, making a total of nearly half as much again as the weight of the Berkeley itself. The effect of this on the b.h.p. per ton figure—with a power output of a modest 18.2 b.h.p.—would be unfair to the car on test. More orthodox small cars weigh about 16 cwt. and have much more power; they can stand extra weight without reflecting its effect markedly in reduced performance.

The power unit of the Berkeley is the Excelsior twin two-stroke, which, fitted with the optional cylinder heads giving 8.2 to 1 compression instead of 7.4, develops 18.2 b.h.p. at 5,250 r.p.m. In the Berkeley's earliest days it was

The luggage locker has its own lid, which conforms to the shape of the tail. No bumpers are fitted at front or rear, partly to keep down the weight and also because it would be extremely difficult to make such fittings robust on this lightweight machine

An alternative version of the car has the head lamps recessed into the wings. The small size can be appreciated when it is realised that the left side of the car is no farther from the kerb than that of the average parked vehicle

Berkeley Sports . . .

thought that the engine should give 18 b.h.p. with the lower compression ratio, but this did not prove to be the case. The capacity is 328 c.c., and the fuel mixture is half a pint of oil to one gallon of petrol. The engine is air cooled. A feature of this unit's performance is the smoothness at any speed, and flexibility which permits top to be used from as little as 12 m.p.h. without snatch. This considerably eases driving in town, as the low speed torque is sufficient to enable the car to hold its place in slow traffic streams with little gear changing. There is no free-wheel, but on the over-run only a soft popping sound indicates that the engine is a two-stroke; there is no jerkiness to call for use of a lower gear even at very low speeds.

Starting was good, hot or cold. A motor cycle type of choke, with its lever under the facia, was required only for a short time after starting from cold. Throughout the test the slow running remained steady, the engine never petering out in traffic hold-ups. Some misfiring did occur on the open road, but it was overcome by attention to the contact-breaker fitted to the end of the generator-starter unit, and reached through a hole in the panelling near the right front wheel.

The maximum speed has already been mentioned; no more need be said except to point out that any car which can sustain 60 m.p.h. and more will never be left behind in any traffic stream on average British main roads. Unlike a number of rival miniature cars, the Berkeley's acceleration from rest (one up) is so good that it can beat many models with engines of twice and even three times the size, including some quantity-produced Eights and Tens. For example, the little car covers a quarter mile from a standing start in 25.6sec, reaches 30 m.p.h. in 8.7sec, 50 m.p.h. in

22.2sec, and 60 m.p.h. in 38.3sec. This is performance of a high order for any small car, and substantiates the makers' designation of the car as a baby "sports."

At high speed the engine feels as if it is working hard. It is certainly revving, for at 60 m.p.h. the r.p.m. is a little over 5,000. Of course, being a ported two-stroke, the engine is free of valve gear, and this enables high r.p.m. to be achieved without risk of serious damage. The noise level is considerable; indeed, when the engine is pulling hard the driver has the kind of noise in his ears associated with a sports-racing car in full stride. The exhaust note is crisp and clean, however, with a tone that is invigorating rather than enervating.

The gear box is mounted at the rear of the engine and transmits power via an enclosed primary chain to the gear box and thence by open chain to the differential and short drive shafts to the front wheels. The front wheel drive suffers from none of the ill-effects which can accompany such a layout; this is due in part to the light weight and low power output of this model. There is no appreciable shake at the steering wheel even when the throttle is opened fully at low speeds on first or second gears, and on corners it matters little whether or not the throttle is open or closed.

Above: The bonnet lid opens with a key, and has a smoothly moulded centre section which rises to a rearward facing louvre. The car tested had fully exposed head lamps, below which are combined side lights and winking indicators. Left: The hood folds away out of sight behind the seat. There is a pleasing simplicity about the glass fibre body

The design of the seat cushion and backrest is ingenious. A thin layer of padding is supported by adjustable straps of strong rubber. The limited luggage space is reduced when the hood and side screens are stowed

The position of the gear lever has been changed from the steering column to the floor, and its in-line motor cycle-type action, although unusual compared with similarly placed levers in orthodox cars, is smooth and easy. Reverse is farthest away from the driver, then comes an intermediate neutral followed by first, main neutral, second, neutral and top. When the car is at standstill, first and reverse gears can be a trifle difficult to engage; that is, the lever on occasions must be moved forward or back, as the case may be, twice or thrice before the gear engages. On the move all changes are easy, and gears may be obtained with or without double declutching. The lever may be whipped from second to top as fast as the driver can move his hand.

One of the best techniques for smooth, fast downward changes is a straight-through action, with the throttle kept partly open. The engine is so responsive that very fast changes may also be made with the full double declutch action, and there is little serious protest if the gear box is treated as one with full synchromesh.

Steering and suspension are usually subject to some criticism on very small cars, but in these respects, as in acceleration, braking and appearance, the Berkeley is particularly good. The steering mechanism works through an orthodox box and transmits little shock. It is light and sensitive, and a steady line may be held on corners taken at relatively high speed. The suspension is firm, but harshness is commendably slight, having in mind the very light sprung weight and the "large" 12in wheels. The handling as a whole has a distinctively sports character which puts the car in a high class within its own speed range. In spite of the front wheel drive the turning circle is quite tolerable at 29ft (right) and 26ft 6in (left). Only $2\frac{1}{4}$ turns of the wheel are required from lock to lock.

Braking efficiency is measured during Road Tests with a Tapley meter, and it is remarkable that this little car is the first to have recorded—time after time—100 per cent. With the combination of 65 sq in of lining area, and due credit to the "slicey" Michelin tyres, this maximum efficiency could be obtained from the hydraulic system with no more than 50 lb load on the pedal—in other words, effort that would be considered quite mild by women drivers. There was no pull to either side, and the wheels did not lock suddenly or viciously. Nor did they grab when hot or cold, or fade in any circumstance. The hand brake appeared at first to be a little too powerful. as pulling the orthodox umbrella, under-facia handle in the ordinary way could lock the rear wheels immediately. One quickly gets used to using the lever gently, and the results are as good or better than most of the positive brake levers widely used before the war.

The driving position must be very low in such a car; in the Berkeley it is achieved partly by clever seat design. The seat cushion and backrest is of very thin padding, supported by adjustable rubber strips. Thus the surface of the bench-type seat cushion is little higher than the floor, yet is comfortable. Its firmness does not give rise to discomfort on long journeys. The wheel is conveniently placed at half arms' reach and the speedometer is directly in front of the driver. The facia panel is austere having, in addition to the speedometer, no more than seven buttons or switches. From left to right these are for the lights, the purposeful horn, ignition, starter, panel light, twin electric wipers and winking indicators. The choke, already mentioned, is under the facia. When driving, one finds that the car feels quite normal; there is none of the feeling experienced, for example, in other lightweight transport such as a motor cycle and sidecar.

As the engine is air-cooled there is no provision for a heater, but some warmth does find its way from the engine compartment to the cockpit. Leg room is ample. The screen is effectively defrosted externally in cold weather

The twin-cylinder 328 c.c. Excelsior two-stroke is now the standard engine. It is available with either of two compression ratios. Between the fuel tank and engine can be seen the Amal carburettor, clutch and gear box, and the housing of the chain drive from the crankshaft to the gear box. On the right of the engine is the dynamo and starter unit

by warm air from the engine compartment which emerges from a rearward facing louvre in the bonnet. In humid conditions the inside of the screen does tend to mist over.

When the car is completely open the current of air blows the hatless driver's hair flat over his face, but there is complete freedom from any buffeting by the wind. With the hood and sidescreens in position the weather protection is good. The only opening available is in the lower edge of the driver's side screen. Its design is such that signalling by hand is a little difficult.

Entry and exit are not easy even when the car is completely open. The simplest way to get in is merely to step

The central gear change now available operates smoothly. There are few instruments and controls. There is a parcels shelf under the facia, and room for oddments in the doors

over the low side and, as far as the driver is concerned, wriggle the legs down beneath the steering wheel. When the car is closed the process is more difficult, and both entry and exit are complicated by the intrusion of glass fibre braces which strengthen the scuttle structure but which, because they lie at right angles to the centre line of the car, impede the feet as they are swung in or out. When getting out at a high kerb, the driver finds himself having to rise from a sitting position which is at about the same level as the pavement; the doors have, however, the merit of clearing the obstruction of the kerbs themselves.

Luggage accommodation is almost non-existent, although there is a little room behind the seats, in the compartment largely occupied in fine weather by the folded-down hood. Under the facia is a wide, deep tray capable of carrying parcels in addition to oddments. A higher lip on its edge would be desirable.

The fuel tank holds 3½ gallons—a maximum normal range of from 142 to 190 miles according to the way in which the car is driven. The absence of fuel gauge *and* any reserve is a fault. The higher engine compression version of the car tested, which runs with a richer mixture, provided an overall figure of about 45 m.p.g., which could be greatly exceeded with ease on any occasion on which the model was used for pottering. If the performance is used to the full, the m.p.g. does suffer.

Engine accessibility on the whole is much better than that of the average orthodox car, and as there is no valve gear, sump, water cooling, and so on, maintenance is reduced to a minimum.

This Berkeley has proved to be much more than an economy runabout. It is a delightful miniature sports car, with characteristics which would do credit to much more powerful and expensive machines. It generously rewards the efforts of drivers who have a feeling for machinery, yet remains so simple in its controls that the most inexperienced drivers would have no difficulty in going from one place to another in complete safety.

BERKELEY SPORTS

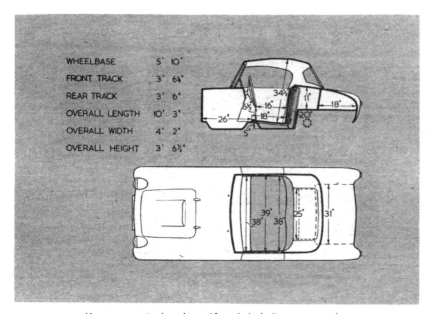

WHEELBASE	5' 10"
FRONT TRACK	3' 6½"
REAR TRACK	3' 6"
OVERALL LENGTH	10'. 3"
OVERALL WIDTH	4' 2"
OVERALL HEIGHT	3' 6½"

Measurements in these ¼in to 1ft scale body diagrams are taken with the driving seat in the central position of fore and aft adjustment and with the seat cushions uncompressed

—————— DATA ——————

PRICE (basic), with two-seater sports body, £382 8s 6d.
British purchase tax, £192 11s 3d.
Total (in Great Britain), £574 19s 9d.

ENGINE: Capacity: 328 c.c. (20.0 cu in).
Number of cylinders: 2.
Bore and stroke: 58 × 62 mm (2.28 × 2.44in).
Two-stroke.
Compression ratio: 8.2 to 1.
B.H.P.: 18.2 at 5,250 r.p.m. (B.H.P. per ton laden 46.7).
Torque: 21.6 lb ft at 3,000 r.p.m.
M.P.H. per 1,000 r.p.m. on top gear, 11.7.

WEIGHT (with 3½ gals fuel): 6¼ cwt (700 lb).
Weight distribution (per cent): F, 62; R, 38.
Laden as tested: 7¾ cwt (864 lb).
Lb per c.c. (laden): 2.6.

BRAKES: Type: Girling.
Method of operation: Hydraulic.
Drum dimensions: F, 7in diameter; 1¼in wide. R, 7in diameter; 1¼in wide.
Lining area: F, 32½ sq in. R, 32½ sq. in (167 sq in per ton laden).

TYRES: 5.20—12in.
Pressures (lb sq in): F, 14; R, 12 (normal).

TANK CAPACITY: 3½ Imperial gallons.

TURNING CIRCLE: 26ft 6in (R) 29ft (L).
Steering wheel turns (lock to lock): 2¼.

DIMENSIONS: Wheelbase: 5ft 10in.
Track: F, 3ft 6½in; R, 3ft 6in.
Length (overall): 10ft 3in.
Height: 3ft 6½in.
Width: 4ft 2in.
Ground clearance: 7in.
Frontal area: 12 sq ft (approximately).

ELECTRICAL SYSTEM: 12 - volt; 22 ampère-hour battery.
Head lights: Double dip; 24-watt bulbs.

SUSPENSION: Front, wishbones with Girling spring and damper units. Rear, swing axles with Girling spring and damper units.

—————— PERFORMANCE (DRIVER ONLY) ——————

ACCELERATION: from constant speeds.
Speed Range, Gear Ratios and Time in sec.

M.P.H.	5.27 to 1	8.43 to 1	13.85 to 1
10—30	—	7.7	—
20—40	13.0	8.2	—
30—50	16.1	—	—
40—60	23.5	—	—

From rest through gears to:

M.P.H.	sec.
30	8.7
50	22.2
60	38.3

Standing quarter mile, 25.6 sec.

SPEEDS ON GEARS:

Gear		M.P.H. (normal and max.)	K.P.H. (normal and max.)
Top	(mean)	65	104.6
	(best)	65	104.6
2nd		28—41	45.1—66.0
1st		14—25	22.5—40.2

TRACTIVE RESISTANCE: 40 lb per ton at 10 M.P.H.

TRACTIVE EFFORT:

	Pull (lb per ton)	Equivalent Gradient
Top	180	1 in 12.4
Second	300	1 in 7.4

BRAKES (from 30 m.p.h. in neutral):

Efficiency	Pedal Pressure (lb)
40 per cent	20
83 per cent	40
100 per cent	50

FUEL CONSUMPTION:
44.7 m.p.g. overall for 318 miles (6.3 litres per 100 km.)
Approximate normal range 40.5—54.0 m.p.g. (7.0—5.2 litres per 100 km.)
Fuel, premium, with 1 part in 16 oil.

WEATHER: Dry; very slight breeze.
Air temperature 52 deg. F.
Acceleration figures are the means of several runs in opposite directions.
Tractive effort and resistance obtained by Tapley meter.
Model described in *The Autocar* of 14 September 1956.

SPEEDOMETER CORRECTION: M.P.H.

Car speedometer				10	20	30	40	50	60	67
True speed				10	20	30	40	49	58	65

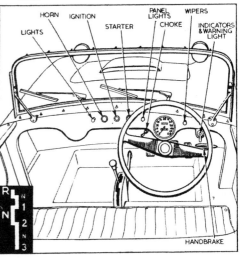

We drive the Berkeley, find it a . . .

MINIATURE MASTERPIECE

So perfectly proportioned is the Berkeley that its tiny size is scarcely apparent without some means of comparison. With hood erected, driver has lots of room. Note massive brake drums, soft-riding Michelin tyres.

FIVE years ago an Englishman named Laurie Bond dreamed up the idea of producing a moulded miniature sports car, with its body and chassis made from fibreglass plastic.

Fortunately, Laurie Bond, an old hand at light car design, is no pipedreamer. His design exceeded expectations and was later adopted by Britain's largest manufacturers of caravans — a logical step since they are also the leading exponent of fibreglass construction in that country.

The new car was named the Berkeley.

Last week, "WHEELS" jumped into Australia's first Berkeley, a pilot model loaned us by John Crouch Motors, of Sydney. The run was one of the most exhilarating and certainly the most unusual we have experienced in many a year. Unfortunately, the bright blue car had scarcely wiped the factory dust off its Michelin tyres and we had to restrain the engine to the manufacturer's recommendation. So our impressions here are published without cold figures, for these will be taken when the speedometer shows a few more miles and will be recorded in a full road test of the Berkeley to be published soon.

So even though we could not blast the car around our test course, we parted company with it with the indelible conviction that not only is the Berkeley a miniature, it is a masterpiece!

It is a true sports car in all senses of the word. Beautifully proportioned, its body looks the part. Magnificently engineered, it holds its line on tight corners like a stubborn leech. In the city it snorts away from the lights with the exuberance of a playful kitten and on the road the engine settles down to a contented burble which reels off mile after mile.

Having said this much, we begin to run out of superlatives, but not quite. The brakes stop the car as though a giant hand has grabbed it from behind. The steering is as true as the note of a concert piano, and the Berkeley is one of the very few cars we have ever encountered which will practically turn a figure-of-eight in a normal width road!

Then in the wildest of city traffic, the car will perkily play ducks and drakes with superb safety. And when the driver wants to park, he has merely to look for the proverbial three-penny piece space.

The car's sporting appearance is unmistakeable. The headlights are

recessed into the wings in true Le-Mans style, the tail sweeps to a graceful curve, and the driver can trail his hand along the road should he feel so inclined, so low is the Berkeley.

To enter the car, you climb through a full sized door and execute a manoeuvre untechnically known as a down-and-wiggle. This brings your stern squarely onto a softly sprung bench seat which is far more comfortable than its spartan appearance suggests.

Directly ahead is an attractive instrument panel, dominated completely by a speedometer calibrated to 120 m.p.h. Alongside it is a fuel gauge and a little to the left, a clock. Grouped below are four control knobs and two push buttons.

We entered the car in the fashion described and stretched the editorial limbs. Surprisingly, leg room is abundant. Then we took a deep breath and discovered that two well upholstered adults can sit comfortably side by side, regardless of whether they breathe in or out of unison.

Once installed in the Berkeley, the driver knows immediately that he is in a sports car. The pistol type handbrake falls to hand for immediate action. The foot controls are

"Wheels" was first in Australia to put a pressman behind the Berkeley's controls. All we can say is—wait for our full road test, upcoming soon, 'cause this little dream car is good, good, GOOD!

well placed. Seating is snug and extremely low. The windscreen is cunningly arranged so that its left hand support serves as a hand grip for the passenger. Our passenger was soon clutching this panic bar fervently.

A touch of the button and the 12-volt Dynastarter whirled into action. The engine fired and turned over smoothly with a crisp burble from the exhaust. First gear is selected from a quadrant placed on the left of the steering column. The throttle is kicked down slightly, for the engine has a light flywheel and needs plenty of r.p.m. to get the car away.

Then the Berkeley slid quietly away, its engine revving happily and healthily. Second gear meant another flick of the lever and the revs built up again quickly. As the engine note rises, so the exhaust burble changes into an angry snarl in true sports car fashion. A change to top and the engine note settled down. The car romped along showing surprising flexibility for a stiff, tight engine, and was undaunted by moderately severe main road hills.

All this from 322 c.c.!

There is no doubt that the Berkeley is factory-trained to point its nose towards the open road, for it is there that her manners are outstanding. The steering is light and direct, with almost neutral steering characteristics and a preciseness which is wholly delightful.

Soon we had the car nosing into corners at speeds which would have invoked loud squeals of impossibility from much more expensive — and brawny — sports cars. But the little Berkeley took every corner with such engaging serenity that we were encouraged to keep up the pressure until the inevitable breakaway point was found. But we resisted temptation. Like we said, the car had scarcely wiped the factory dust off her tyres and we felt honour bound to respect the manufacturers' wishes. Besides, we're going to road test it later, remember?

One of the really outstanding qualities of the Berkeley is that it corners almost entirely without roll. Its stability is unbelievable, and how much of this can be attributed to front wheel drive design is a matter for conjecture. The plain fact is that the car rolls round really tight corners like they weren't there.

The suspension is medium to firm. The Berkeley rides over tram lines, pot holes and miscellaneous road debris with a tranquility born of pedigree breeding.

It was soon abundantly clear that the Berkeley has the suspension and road manners of a true 100 m.p.h. sports car, and, although its little engine doesn't appear to have the punch to yield neck-snapping acceleration, its powerful hydraulic

brakes would be outstanding on any Grand Prix car.

These brakes have 7" diameter drums and are made by Girling. The front have two leading shoes, the rear a leading and a trailing shoe. Since the car weighs only a modest 6 cwt., the friction area per ton is quite phenomenal, and stopping power therefore is prodigious.

Undoubtedly the passenger will need prior warning if any major braking operation is about to be launched, otherwise he may be catapulted out of the car like a jet pilot's ejection seat!

The power unit is a specially tuned British Anzani air-cooled twin cylinder two stroke engine, developing 15 b.h.p. at 5,000 r.p.m. Other cars coming here are to be fitted with the similarly sized Excelsior Talisman. We understand that the makers are considering adopting a 600 c.c. twin cylinder, four-stroke engine with a 30 b.h.p. up its sleeve.

Then—whew!!!

At present a three speed gearbox with commendable synchromesh is fitted. Some practice is required to manipulate it deftly, since, being a motor cycle type, there is a neutral between each gear. But although the three gears give adequate performance, one cannot help wondering just how soon enthusiasts will be clamouring for a close ratio four speed box as an extra.

The general design of the chassis and mechanical layout have already been covered in "WHEELS", but a

thorough examination of the car we drove strengthened our impression that the design is unusually tidy and brilliantly worked out.

The car's all-weather equipment is unique. The hood must be one of the very few genuine one-man designs in captivity. Erection is quick and the design is so simple that one wonders why no one else had thought of a pair of collapsible supports which dove-tail into each other. Another ingenious idea is that the large rear window is made from plastic and is bonded direct to the plastic hood. It can be sat on, twisted, smitten, or wrinkled, and comes out smiling.

On this note, we can round off by repeating ourselves. The Berkeley is a masterpiece in miniature. If the manufacturers had built its road manners into a full-sized car selling at twice the price, the sporting public would still have been delighted. As it is, they are offering 60 m.p.g. motoring, a lively road performance, and delightful handling characteristics built into a diminutive car which will undersell every other sports car in Australia by a sizeable margin.

Throw in superb steering and brakes, and a top speed said to be 70 m.p.h., and you have a thoroughbred vehicle which must truly be one of the safest cars ever designed, regardless of size or horsepower.

What more need we say, except . . . wait, just wait for that road test! ●

Hood down, the Berkeley retains its trim appearance. 5'11" "Wheels" man fits in cockpit comfortably, with lots of room for a hefty passenger. Windscreen frame stay doubles as a passenger "panic bar".

the *Roadster* _____ ... BY BERKELEY

BOTH MODELS

DIMENSIONS: Wheelbase 5 ft. 10 in. Track 3 ft. 8 in. Overall length 10 ft. 3 in. Overall width 4 ft. 2 in. Ground clearance 5 in. Turning circle 28 ft. Weight 6 cwt.

BODY AND FRAME: Resin bonded moulded glass fibre with aluminium alloy bulkheads and cross members moulded in to form a single structure.

COUPE MODEL: Fixed hard top with built in windshield and rear window.

SUSPENSION: All wheels independently sprung. Front by unequal length wishbones with Girling coil springs and damper units. Rear by swing axles with Girling coil spring and damper unit.

STEERING: Burman worm and nut steering box with three piece divided track rod and 16 in. steering wheel.

CONTROLS: Gear change lever mounted centrally on floor. Clutch, brake and accelerator pedals of pendant design; pistol type hand brake.

BRAKES: 7 in. Gibling hydraulic. Front, two leading shoes; rear, one leading and one trailing shoe.

WHEELS: Lightweight wheels with 5 stud fixing; fitted with 5.20 x 12 Michelin tires.

ELECTRICAL EQUIPMENT: 12 volt battery, charged by Siba Dynastarter. Ignition by twin coils. Two headlamps, incorporating parking lights, two tail lamps, incorporating hydraulically operated stop lights; two reflectors; twin electrical screen wipers; electric horn.

INSTRUMENTS: 4 in. dia. speedometer with ignition warning light. Head and side light switch, horn button, starter button, fuel gauge, amp. meter, high beam flashing indicator. Switch for windshield wiper attached to wiper motor.

SEATING: Bench type seat upholstered in Vynide.

COLORS: Red, blue, green, with grey upholstery.

STANDARD EQUIPMENT: Lever type jack, set of tools, instruction books.

the *Coupé* _____ ... BY BERKELEY

the BERKELEY has arrived!

ENGINE

Excelsior air cooled twin cylinder two stroke:
capacity 328 c.c.
Bore 58 m.m.:
Stroke 62 m.m.
90 Watt Siba Dynastarter
Output 18 b.h.p. at 5000 r.p.m.

TRANSMISSION

Front wheel drive through differential and three speed reverse gear box. Final drive by roller chain.

492 c.c. MODEL

ENGINE

Exclusive Excelsior air cooled 3 cylinder Two Stroke:
capacity 492 c.c.
Bore 58 m.m.
Stroke 62 m.m.
90 Watt Siba Dynastarter
Output 30 b.p.h. at 5500 r.p.m.

TRANSMISSION

Front wheel drive through differential & four speed & reverse gear box. Gear ratios: 1st—15.21 to 1; 2nd—9.18 to 1; 3rd—6.35 to 1; 4th—4.64 to 1; reverse—16.61 to 1.

INTERNATIONAL COMMENTS:

From The Autocar, the British magazine authority on sports cars:

"One of the best techniques for smooth, fast downward changes is a straight-through action, with the throttle kept partly open. The engine is so responsive that very fast changes may also be made with the full double declutch ation, and there is little serious protest if the gear box is treated as one with full synchromesh."

"Braking efficiency is measured during Road Tests with a Tapley meter, and it is remarkable that this little car is the first to have recorded . . . time after time . . . 100 per cent."

"The screen (windshield) is effectively defrosted externally in cold weather by warm air from the engine compartment which emerges from a rearward facing louvre in the bonnet."

"Engine accessibility on the whole is much better than that of the average orthodox car, and as there is no valve gear, sump, water cooling and so on, maintenance is reduced to a minimum."

RALLIES and DRIVING TESTS

LONDON MOTOR CLUB LTD., BRANDS HATCH SPRINT ON SUNDAY, 18th AUGUST 1957

W. Rosson, driving a 328 c.c. Berkeley was the winner of Group 3—Sports Cars, Class A, up to 1,000 c.c. The sprint was over two laps, and the times were as follows:

Best practice lap: 1 min. 28.8 secs.
First run: 2 min. 50.2 secs.
Second run: 2 min. 53.4 secs.

These times are considerably faster than many entrants driving closed cars in classes up to 2,000 c.c., and we would like to congratulate Mr. Rosson on putting up a first-class show.

DRIVING TESTS, MAIDSTONE AND MID-KENT MOTOR CLUB on 21st JULY, 1957

There were 34 entrants, and the cars were divided into the following classes:

Class A. Open, under 1500 c.c.   Class C. Trials cars.
Class B. Saloon, under 1500 c.c.   Class D. Open, 1500 c.c. and over.
                    Class E. Saloon, 1500 c.c. and over.

Winner of Class A: A. R. Wheeler (Berkeley)
Second in Class A: I. Mantle (Berkeley)
Premier Award, irrespective of class: A. R. Wheeler (Berkeley)

"The Motor," 12th June, 1957

". . . and Goddard-Watts set up a new 350 lap record in a Berkeley coupe at 58.62 m.p.h."

THAMES ESTUARY AUTOMOBILE CLUB SPEED TRIALS AT BRANDS HATCH ON 16th JUNE, 1957

The following were the results for standard sports and standard saloon cars up to 1,000 c.c.:

1. J. I. Goddard-Watts (Berkeley)
                    Time: 2 mins. 45.4 secs.
2. R. A. Jamieson (Berkeley)
                    Time: 2 mins. 47.2 secs.
3. N. W. Graham (Berkeley)
                    Time: 2 mins. 58.4 secs.

DRIVING TEST ORGANIZED BY THE SINGER OWNERS CLUB AT CALIFORNIA IN ENGLAND, WOKINGHAM, ON 16th JUNE, 1957

A privately entered Berkeley was the outright winner of this event.

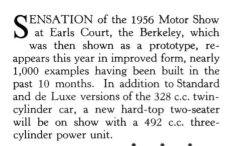

ENLARGED doors with recessed exterior handles are used on the three-cylinder Hard-top model (*left*). Simpler equipment and lack of wheel discs identify the standard version of the two-cylinder car below.

S ENSATION of the 1956 Motor Show at Earls Court, the Berkeley, which was then shown as a prototype, re-appears this year in improved form, nearly 1,000 examples having been built in the past 10 months. In addition to Standard and de Luxe versions of the 328 c.c. twin-cylinder car, a new hard-top two-seater will be on show with a 492 c.c. three-cylinder power unit.

* * *

Major change in the twin-cylinder Berkeley since its introduction has been the adoption of the 328 c.c. Excelsior two-stroke engine in place of the 322 c.c. unit of a different make used in early production models. For the coming season, two versions of this engine are to be offered, standard cars having a single Amal carburetter and de Luxe examples using a pair of Amal carburetters to gain enhanced performance. From this engine, an enclosed chain transmits power to an Albion multi-plate clutch in unit with a three-speed and reverse gearbox, and an open chain transmits power to the differential which drives the front wheels through universally jointed shafts.

Also of Excelsior make, the new 492 c.c. engine illustrated on these pages has been designed to use the same moving parts as the twin-cylinder unit, and when develop-

ment work is complete is expected to deliver at least 50% more power than does the smaller engine. Two-up, a Berkeley with the first experimental example of this engine mated temporarily to a three-speed gearbox was timed from rest to 50 m.p.h. in just under 15 seconds and exceeded 70 m.p.h. (as a timed two-way average) by an appreciable margin, in the hands of members of the staff of *The Motor*: production versions will have a four-speed gearbox.

As may be seen from the drawing, this two-stroke engine uses individual air-cooled cylinders, and the design of the separate compression-tight crankcases requires a built-up crankshaft which is supported on three roller bearings and one ball bearing. Flat-topped pistons each carry two compression rings (no scraper rings are needed with petroil lubrication) and ports uncovered by the upper and lower edges of each piston control the intake of

	328 c.c.	492 c.c.			328 c.c.	492 c.c.
Engine dimensions			**Chassis details**			
Cylinders	2 (air cooled)	3 (air cooled)	Brakes	Girling hydraulic (2 l.s. front)	Girling hydraulic (2 l.s. front)
Bore	58 mm.	58 mm.	Brake drum diameter...	7-in.	7-in.
Stroke	62 mm.	62 mm.	Friction lining area ...	65 sq. in.	65 sq. in.
Cubic capacity ...	328 c.c.	492 c.c.	Suspension :		
Piston area	8.2 sq. in.	12.3 sq. in.	Front	Coil and wishbone I.F.S.	Coil and wishbone I.F.S.
Valves	None (2-stroke)	None (2-stroke)	Rear	Coil and divided axle I.R.S.	Coil and divided axle I.R.S.
Compression ratio ...	7.4	7.5	Shock absorbers ...	Girling telescopic	Girling telescopic
Engine performance			Wheel type	Removable rims	Removable rims
Max. power	18 b.h.p.	—	Tyre size	5.20-12	5.20-12
at	5,000 r.p.m.	—	Steering gear	Burman worm and nut	Burman worm and nut
Max. b.m.e.p. ...	81 lb./sq. in. × 2 (2-stroke)	—	**Dimensions**		
at	3,000 r.p.m.	—	Wheelbase	5 ft. 10 in.	5 ft. 10 in.
B.H.P. per sq. in. piston area	2.20	—	Track: front and rear	3 ft. 6 in.	3 ft. 6 in.
Piston speed at max. power	2,030	—	Overall length ...	10 ft. 3 in.	10 ft. 3 in.
Engine details			Overall width ...	4 ft. 2 in.	4 ft. 2 in.
Carburetter	Amal (2 on de luxe model)	3 Amal	Overall height ...	3 ft. 6½ in.	3 ft. 6½ in.
Ignition timing control	fixed	fixed	Ground clearance ...	5 in.	5 in.
Plugs: make and type	K.L.G. type FE.70.D	K.L.G. type FE.70.D	Turning circle ...	left 26½ ft., right 29 ft.	left 26½ ft., right 29 ft.
Fuel pump	Gravity feed	S.U. electrical	Dry weight	6 cwt.	6¼ cwt.
Fuel capacity	3½ gallons	3½ gallons	**Performance factors**		
Oil filter	None (petroil lubrication)	None (petroil lubrication)	(at dry weight)		
Cooling system ...	Air	Air	Piston area, sq. in. per ton	27.4	39.3
Electrical system ...	12-volt Siba dynamotor	12-volt Siba dynamotor	Brake lining area, sq. in. per ton	216	208
Transmission			Top gear m.p.h. per 1,000 r.p.m.	11.8	14.5
Clutch	Albion multi-plate	Albion multi-plate	Top gear m.p.h. per 1,000 ft./min. piston speed...	34.0	41.6
Gear ratios:			Litres per ton-mile ...	2,780	3,260
Top	5.7	4.65			
3rd	—	6.41			
2nd	8.43	9.20			
1st	13.85	15.25			
Rev.	17.25	16.65			
Prop. shaft	None (front drive)	None (front drive)			
Final drive	Chain	Chain			

THREE-CYLINDER BERKELEY

EXTRA performance will be available when this three-cylinder Excelsior engine goes into production, a built-up crankshaft going with the compression-tight individual crankcases. Transverse mounting ahead of the driven front wheels provides adequate natural air cooling.

mixture to the crankcase from the carburetter, transfer of lightly compressed mixture from the crankcase to the cylinder, and exhaust of spent charge from the cylinder. Ignition is by three separate coils and a triple contact-breaker.

To exploit the full potentialities of the larger engine, 3-cylinder Berkeley cars will have a new 4-speed and reverse gearbox of Albion make, a drawing of which appears on these pages, instead of the 3-speed and reverse pattern used on the 2-cylinder cars. No synchromesh is used, but as the inertia of the multi-plate clutch is small and the clutch-gearbox unit runs at less than half engine speed the dog-engaged ratios should be easy to select. All cars now have a floor-mounted central gear lever, replacing one on the steering column.

Apart from some early difficulties with surface finish, the resin-bonded glass fibre body-chassis unit of the Berkeley has given excellent results, making possible the astonishingly low weight of only 6 cwt. for the complete car. Moulded in the Berkeley factory at Biggleswade, the punt-type underframe has certain vital reinforcement plates moulded into it and is further stiffened by aluminium pressings rivetted to it. Suspension is independent for all four wheels, by transverse parallelogram linkages at the front and by swinging half-axles at the rear, in conjunction with four Girling suspension units which have coil springs encircling telescopic damper units. The wheels comprise light steel 12-inch rims with

5-stud attachment to the drums of 7-inch Girling hydraulic brakes. Steering is by a Burman gear, in conjunction with which an idler arm and three-piece track rod are used to ensure steering accuracy.

At a basic price of only £332 7s. 6d. (plus purchase tax) the twin-cylinder "standard" Berkeley is offered as a two-seater complete with hood, twin screen wipers, speedometer, tool kit, Siba combined dynamo and starter, etc., but without a spare wheel and tyre. Priced at £382 8s. 6d. (plus purchase tax) the de Luxe version has such additional features as the spare wheel and tyre, plated wheel discs with dummy knock-on caps, ammeter, fuel contents gauge, direction indicators, sidescreens, twin carburetters, and many refinements of interior and exterior trim. A removable hard-top can be supplied for either.

A fresh version of the Berkeley body is fitted to the 3-cylinder cars, with a more permanent hard-top, wider doors carrying sliding side windows, recessed external door handles, and a curved rear window of large area.

The basic prices of the 3-cylinder cars range from £381 15s. 4d. for a standard tourer to £448 8s. 0d. for the de luxe coupé.

COMPACT layout of the four-speed and reverse gearbox, which is chain driven from the engine, is secured by making the mainshaft and layshaft gears slide together, the layshaft having pegs which engage with the appropriate gears for the indirect forward ratios.

ACCESS to luggage space behind the bench seat of the de Luxe twin-cylinder model is now through a front-hinged panel.

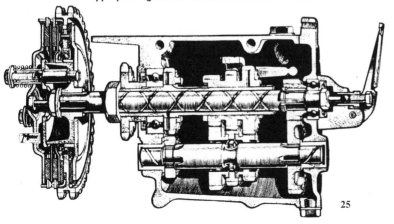

25

	U.K. Basic			UK Total including P.T.		
	£	s	d	£	s	d
328 c.c. model						
Standard soft top	332	7	6	499	18	3
Standard coupé	348	5	6	523	15	0
De luxe soft top	382	8	6	574	19	9
De luxe coupé	398	8	0	598	19	0
492 c.c. model						
Standard soft top	381	15	4	573	19	10
Standard coupé	397	14	7	597	18	11
De luxe soft top	432	9	0	650	0	0
De luxe coupé	448	8	0	673	19	0

Right: the new Berkeley coupé provides good all-round visibility and, in the de luxe form, has wheel discs with imitation "knock-off" hub caps. Below: entry is reasonably easy. The gear change is of the motor-cycle type, with central lever

New 3-cylinder Engine for The Berkeley

FIXED-HEAD COUPÉ ADDED

TO THE RANGE

IMPORTANT additions to the Berkeley programme have been announced for 1958: an in-line, air-cooled 3-cylinder two-stroke engine evolved by the Excelsior company, will be made available as an alternative to the 2-cylinder unit; in addition, a coupé body had been included in the range.

In effect there will now be a choice of four models, each available in standard or de luxe form. These are the open sports and the coupé, with either the 328 c.c. twin-cylinder Excelsior two-stroke or the new 3-cylinder unit. All models have independent suspension of all wheels, at the front by unequal wishbones and at the rear by swing axles, with Girling coil spring and damper units on all wheels. The bodies, of resin-bonded glass fibre, have aluminium alloy bulk-heads and cross members moulded in.

De luxe models have superior trim, the intake grille plated, the operating rod from the centrally placed gear lever covered in, winking indicators, and spun aluminium alloy wheel discs with imitation knock-off hub caps. There is also a larger speedometer on the de luxe cars, and an ignition warning light, flanked by an ammeter and a fuel level gauge.

The new coupé is an attractive little car, with good visibility all round, and reasonable ease of entry and exit, having in mind the model's small overall dimensions. While the open car has door handles only on the inside, on the coupé recesses have been made for the exterior handles in the lower part of the door mouldings. Frontal treatment of the models is now a little different, the grille having a square pattern instead of the earlier diamond shape.

SPECIFICATION

ENGINE: (New Excelsior unit): No. of cylinders, 3 in line; Bore and stroke, 58 x 62 mm (2.283 x 2.441in); Displacement, 492 c.c. (30 cu in); Valve position, ported two-stroke; Compression ratio, 7.5 to 1; Max b.h.p. (gross), 30 at 5,500 r.p.m.; Carburation three 376/9 Amals; Tank capacity, 3½ Imp. gal. (16 litres); Cooling system, air-cooled; Battery, 12 volt 23 amp hr.

TRANSMISSION: Clutch, Albion multiplate; Gear box, Albion; Overall gear ratios, Top 4.64; 3rd, 6.35; 2nd, 9.18; 1st, 15.21; reverse, 16.61 to 1; Final drive, chain, 2.23 to 1.

CHASSIS: Brakes, Girling hydraulic; Drum dia, shoe width, 7 x 1¼in; Suspension: front, unequal wishbones; rear, swinging arms; Dampers, Girling telescopic combined with coil springs; Wheels, disc; Tyre size, 5.20—12in; Steering, Burman worm and nut; Steering wheel, two-spoke, 16in dia; Turns, lock to lock, 2¼.

DIMENSIONS: Wheelbase, 5ft 10in (178 cm); Track: front, 3ft 8in (112 cm); rear, 3ft 8in (112 cm); Overall length, 10ft 3in (312 cm); Overall width, 4ft 2in (127 cm); Overall height (unladen), 3ft 7½in (110 cm); Minimum ground clearance (unladen), 7in (178 mm); Turning circle, L, 26ft 5in (8.1 m); R, 29ft (8.8 m); Kerb weight, 6 cwt (305 kg).

PERFORMANCE DATA: Top gear m.p.h. per 1,000 r.p.m., 13.2; Brake surface area swept by linings, 110 sq in; Weight distribution (kerb weight), F, 65 per cent; R, 35 per cent.

In its 1958 form the open version of the Berkeley is similar to its predecessor except for the square-patterned grille. This is plated on the de luxe version

New 3-cylinder

for

Berkeley . . .

The latest 3-cylinder Excelsior two-stroke engine is installed transversely in the Berkeley. There are three Amal carburettors, behind which can be seen the battery and part of the fuel tank

The three-cylinder engine is basically similar to the 328 c.c. twin Talisman and. in effect, utilizes an additional cylinder of the same size (58 mm bore, 62 mm stroke). It is of the transfer port type, and induction is by three Amal Monobloc carburettors—one to each cylinder.

The crankcase comprises four sections —an end housing at the primary chain side, two centre sections and an end cover to house the Siba Dynastart; this unit is used for starting, as a generator and as a low-tension make-and-break assembly for the three individual coils.

The crankshaft is unusual in being a built-up assembly mounted on three ball and four roller bearings. There is a synthetic rubber seal between each crankcase compartment to eliminate mixture loss during the transfer process.

Firing order is 1, 2, 3, with the crank throws disposed at 120 degrees. Each connecting rod is a solid forging with a double row of uncaged rollers for the big end bearing. The first crank throw is

assembled with the connecting rod and rollers as a unit, into the crankcase halves. The next half crank is then keyed on with its crankpin driven in; the other half of this sub-unit is a sliding fit on its mating journal. No. 6 Witney keys locate each half of the crank journals and they are retained by a sleeve-type nut, which is

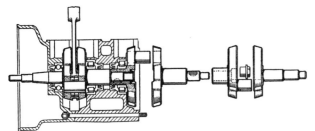

Left: Built-up crankshaft with pressed-in crankpin, showing the disposition of the seven ball and roller bearings. Below: Separate cylinder barrels and heads are used. Close clearances and separate seals reduce transfer losses

locked in position by peening the thread. The last cylinder is a repetition of this process and the assembly technique is thus to thread the crankshaft and crankcase together as assembly proceeds.

Separate cast-iron barrels and light-alloy heads are employed, with common hold-down studs anchored in the crankcase. There is no cylinder head gasket, the fire joint being obtained by a narrow ring around the cylinder bore left slightly proud of the main joint face. Each flat crown piston carries two rings, pegged to prevent rotation, and the gudgeon pins are bushed in the piston with a floating bronze bush in the connecting rod. Combustion chambers are part spherical in form, with a conical blend into the cylinder bore; sparking plugs are inclined away from the exhaust port.

A four-speed Albion gear box, incor-

Continued on page 30

AMAZING LITTLE BERKELEY

Its cornering and braking put racing cars to shame, reports David McKay

I HAVE just logged 515 miles in the first Berkeley Sports to reach Sydney—and I'm astounded at the roadability and endurance of this tiny motorbike-engined two-seater.

Its cornering puts most racing cars to shame. Take that 90-degree left-hander out of Bathurst's Pit Straight, where 50 m.p.h. is generally considered the safe limit. Rounding it at that speed, the Berkeley felt steady as a rock; given a little extra power, I'm sure it would go round at 60 just as easily.

It cruises happily at 45-50 m.p.h.; no amount of ill-treatment can force it to give less than about 60 miles to the gallon; and its braking efficiency is something like 200 percent by normal standards! (I'll explain that later.)

The Berkeley has its faults, too, and these will be duly catalogued—but what a surprise package, all the same!

Getting Acquainted

My introduction to the car took place under most unfavorable conditions. I picked it up from the N.S.W. distributors, John Crouch Motors, at 5 p.m. on the Wednesday before Easter. Sydney's traffic was at its thickest, and getting the Berkeley home through the city and over the Harbor Bridge was no picnic.

Anyone accustomed to motorbikes might have been at home in the car at once, but I certainly wasn't. The notched quadrant gear-change was something I'd never struck before—and then that business of having to rev up madly for each take-off . . .

Relieved to get home in one piece, I took my first good look at the car and decided that photos don't do justice to the delightful lines and general good finish of its fibreglass body.

Engine-room layout is neat and well planned. The engine in this particular car is an Excelsior Talisman twin, and every part of it is accessible; unfortunately data on this new unit hasn't yet reached Australia. The same goes for the Amal carby and other accessories.

GEAR-CHANGE in notched quadrant (as on old-fashioned motorbikes) takes a lot of getting used to, says McKay. Tacho should replace clock.

A very novel feature is the incorporation of the fibreglass body together with the chassis framing, so that they form a unitary structure. The two large-diameter main tubular members are made in two halves—one plastic and one aluminium—bonded and riveted together. There are also aluminium cross-members, and a short aluminium box reinforces the engine compartment.

The Berkeley is the creation of Laurie Bond, who designed the Bond Minicar. It is made by Berkeley Coachwork Ltd., of Biggleswade, Bedfordshire, who are Britain's leading plastic caravan manufacturers—so it's not surprising that they should turn out such a well-constructed fibreglass car body.

The 16-inch steering wheel is well positioned; so are the pendant-type clutch, brake and accelerator pedals, the pistol-grip handbrake and the aforementioned gear-change quadrant.

SPECIFICATIONS

ENGINE: 2-cylinder, 2-stroke; capacity 328 c.c.; max. b.h.p. 17; Amal Carburettor, wet maze filter, Siba dynasterter on crankshaft, gravity petrol feed, 12v. ignition.
TRANSMISSION: f.w.d. through differential and 3-speed gearbox in unit with engine, driven by roller chain.
SUSPENSION: Independent all-round; front by unequal wishbones with Girling combined coil spring and damper units; rear by swing axles with combined units.
STEERING: Burman worm-and-nut; 28ft. turning circle.
WHEELS: Lightweight 5-stud rims; 5.20 by 12in. Michelin tyres.
BRAKES: Girling hydraulic, 7in. diameter; 2 l.s. at front.
CONSTRUCTION: Stressed-skin, with body and frame in one unit.
DIMENSIONS: Wheelbase 5ft. 10in.; track, 3ft. 8in. front and rear; length 10ft. 3in., width 4ft. 2in.; road clearance 5in.
DRY WEIGHT: 5½cwt.
FUEL TANK: 3½ gallons.

PERFORMANCE

CONDITIONS: Warm weather, dry roads; two occupants; premium fuel and 2-stroke oil (16 to 1).
BEST SPEED: 62 m.p.h.
FLYING quarter-mile: 58 m.p.h.
STANDING quarter-mile: 27.5s.
ACCELERATION through gears: 0-20, 5.1s.; 0-30, 10.1s.; 0-40, 16.7s.; 0-50, 27.2s.
ACCELERATION in top: 30-50, 15.0s.; in second: 10-30, 9.8s.
MAXIMUM SPEEDS in indirect gears: First, 25 m.p.h.; second, 45.
BRAKING: 14ft. 6in. to stop from 30 m.p.h.
CONSUMPTION: 59¼ m.p.g. including all tests.

PRICE: £886 with tax

EXCELSIOR twin-cylinder engine is integral with the 3-speed gearbox and drive is on front wheels. BELOW: Spare occupies most of "dicky."

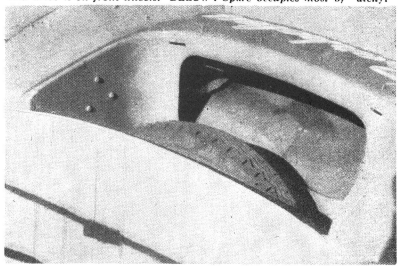

to the left under the steering wheel. The five lever positions give you reverse, neutral, 1st, 2nd and 3rd, in that order.

Behind the cockpit is a "dicky" which houses the spare wheel and has a cubby-hole where the hood and a few odds-and-ends can be stowed. The spare can also be carried on a shelf under the dash, and then a small child or two can be popped into the "dicky."

There are large open pockets on the inside of the two doors. The doors themselves are rather small; if they would only stay open, it would make exit and entrance far easier.

The hood and side-curtains are of very good quality, and erection couldn't be any easier or quicker. The Berkeley is one of the few sports cars whose appearance isn't ruined when the hood is in position—personally, I liked its looks even better with the hood up.

On the Road

Next morning my wife and I set out for Bathurst, 130-odd miles away. The weather was fine, the traffic moderate; I soon found myself getting the hang of the little car and

(Continued overleaf)

29

BERKELEY
Continued from page 29

began to enjoy the drive (though I must admit I still get foxed by the "bike change" occasionally—perhaps a small adjustment would make second gear easier to find).

The cockpit is fairly intimate with two people aboard, to say the least—hurtling round corners, as one does in the Berkeley, tends to land the co-pilot in the driver's lap unless he (or she) has a firm grip. A divided seat would be a big help. The present bench seat is adequate, but its back is pretty rigid; I understand the local agents intend to improve the seating, to suit the longer distances usually travelled in Australia.

With the hood stowed away, vision fore and aft is first-rate; but raising the hood restricts it considerably. The rear-view mirror should be positioned on the scuttle to obtain a better view of following traffic; at present it is set too high, and a following car cannot be seen until it's almost on top of the Berkeley.

For medium-sized adults there is sufficient room, but a tall person finds his head in contact with the hood, and his side-vision is limited.

Driving at night, I found the headlights quite inadequate for the amazing performance of the Berkeley. With more powerful lamps, really good averages could be made during darkness. Likewise, the horn should be shrill and insistent for such a "ducker in-and-out of traffic" as the Berkeley.

The instruments are sparse—a speedo and a petrol gauge. There's a clock as well, which I would like to see replaced by a tachometer. A separate switch cuts off the lighting to the dash, doing away with reflections on the sloped screen.

On long journeys the noise of the two-stroke can become rather tiring, and engine fumes tend to find their way into the cockpit along with dust. This dust problem will doubtless have to be remedied out here, as English manufacturers have no conception of our dirt roads.

Phenomenal Braking

As my familiarity with the Berkeley grew, I found I could take liberties with it which would spell disaster in most cars.

The outstanding features of this little sportster are the brakes and the road-holding. The former work wonderfully—so wonderfully that Ferodo's experts will have to change their "braking table" figures, which rate a 30ft. stop from 30 m.p.h. as 100 percent efficiency. The Berkeley put the braking Tapley meter right off the clock and registered 14ft. 6in. from 30 m.p.h—in other words, it showed more than double the theoretical maximum efficiency!

Later, after we'd coasted down the steep Kurrajong descent on the stoppers, the little car pulled up in 17ft.—still better than Ferodo's chart figures. These phenomenal results are due to good anchors coupled with a kerb weight of only 5½cwt.

The Berkeley driver can outbrake anyone for a corner, and it is often unnecessary to touch the brakes even for a right-angle turn—the handling takes care of it. You just turn the wheel and around you go, 10 m.p.h. faster than anyone else.

Downhill around corners you can pass anything with impunity, and on undulating roads you can hold most cars at bay—although hills soon bring you down to earth, reminding you that the Berkeley's engine is tiny, however willing it may be.

Why is the road-holding so good? The answer is front-wheel drive, coupled with really excellent independent suspension on all four wheels.

Economical, Too

Fuel consumption was ridiculously low. Driven hard all the way to and from Bathurst, punched around Mt. Panorama by anyone who wanted a try, including Stan Jones, Ray Long, and many others, thrashed along through acceleration tests and many laps round Mt. Druitt, the Berkeley produced an overall consumption figure a fraction short of 60 m.p.g. What a normal driver would get, I can't imagine—probably over 65, and maybe as much as 70 m.p.g.

Top speed was around the 60 m.p.h. mark, though I'm told that 70 is "normal" in a fully run-in car. I found 45-50 an easy, comfortable cruising speed.

I feel the Berkeley will fill a need over here. It handles rough dirt roads well (although I don't imagine it would ever win a round-Australia trial—its low ground clearance, among other things, would see to that). Whether Mum will take it shopping or not remains to be seen, for it is not the easiest of cars to drive. On the other hand, economy, performance, and excellent handling are seldom found together in such quantities in one car.

If the price could be cut by a third, through local manufacture, then everyone would want a Berkeley; but at present I feel it's only the enthusiasts who will fill the orders. The greatest scope is for the racing fellow: a 1000 c.c. H.R.D. or 500 c.c. Norton engine would really make the little machine perform—and what a wonderful nursery it would make for the tyros! ● ● ●

Continued from page 27

3-cylinder Berkeley . . .

porating reverse, is bolted to the back face of the crankcase below the carburettor, the engine being mounted transversely in the frame. Primary drive is by a ⅜in pitch Duplex roller chain to a multi-plate clutch running in oil. The chain drive to

the chassis-mounted differential is by an open roller chain.

As the engine is mounted in the front of the car with the exhaust ports pointing forward, it has not been found necessary to use a cooling fan; this results in a useful saving of weight, and the bare engine, less gear box, weighs 98 lb. Cooling fins are deep, which adds to the length

(more precisely width as installed in the Berkeley) so that the unit measures 21in from cover to cover.

Lubrication is by the usual mixture of petrol and oil in the ratio of 16 to 1—considerably more than is used in similar continental engines, many of which are now operating on mixture ratios of between 30 and 40 to 1.

BERKELEY

An interesting sportster, with a two-stroke engine and chain drive

THIS tiny car (its overall length is just over 10 feet—122.5 inches) looks at first glance like an expensive toy. But it is considerably more than that. It can carry two men at over 60 m.p.h., with a very economical consumption of gasoline.

Up to late 1958, the Berkeley had been arriving in the United States with a two-cylinder, two-stroke Excelsior of 328 cc. capacity. It is now equipped with a three-cylinder Excelsior of 492 cc. Bore and stroke are the same; the power output has been increased to 30 horsepower at 5,500 r.p.m. Three Amal carburetors are fitted.

The drive is to the front wheels, and the engine is mounted ahead of the wheels—always an advantage in front-wheel drive, since it helps the traction on steep uphill grades. The starter and generator are one (Siba Dynastart). The gearbox is of the motorcycle type, with three speeds (and, of course, reverse); the shift lever (quadrant type) is on the steering column. Final drive is by chain.

The Berkeley's body is of plastic, reinforced with light metal alloy. The seats are unusual—the thin upholstery cushions which are supported on wide bands of rubber, which are easily adjustable to allow for a light or heavy rider. The driver is carried very low to the ground (total height, with the top up, is only 43.5 inches!). Despite the miniature dimensions, two six-footers can sit side by side, though a slight sidewise position on the part of the passenger is needed to give shoulder room to the driver.

The engine and gearbox are easily accessible when the hood is raised, and maintenance should be simple. The spare wheel can be carried on a large shelf up front in case its space behind the seats is wanted for luggage.

The hollow tail of the car is used for stowing the top, tonneau cover and jack. There is added space in the door pockets and a shelf under the dash. All in all, a very interesting and deserving little automobile.

Roadtest Summary: PLUS—Since most people are not over-six-footers, seating comfort is quite adequate for touring in the Berkeley.

The engine starts silently and at once; it answers immediately to the throttle. The gearshift is positive in its action. Thanks to its low silhouette and good suspension, the car's roadholding characteristics are up to a very high standard of excellence. On corners, as is usual with front-wheel-drive, the car hugs the road if power is kept applied. Roll is almost nonexistent. The ride is surprisingly comfortable, including rough road surface. There are no rattles in the body. The top is completely waterproof, even in driving rain.

The steering is light and positive. The pulling power of the engine, despite its only 18 h.p. output, is quite adequate. The brakes, being exposed through the perforated wheel discs, do not heat up.

Acceleration: Zero to 30 m.p.h.—10.5 seconds; zero to 50 m.p.h.—31 seconds. Top speed, 65 m.p.h. Mileage, 50-65 m.p.g.

MINUS—As with other two-stroke engines, the idle is rough. The exhaust is noisy; more so as the speed increases. The exhaust pipe is forward of the seating compartment, where it makes its presence especially known.

The steering becomes stiff as the wheels are locked over to their most extreme angle, a trait in common with most front-wheel-drive automobiles.

Leaning too far forward or back in his seat, a tall driver will find his head touching the frames of the top. •

Built very low to the ground, the Berkeley is extremely stable, hugs the round on the curves.

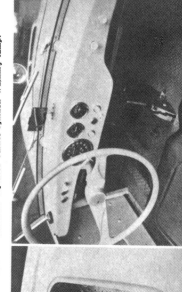

View of cockpit. Gearshift is motorcycle type. Ammeter replaces earlier ignition warning lamp.

The coupe version. A smart looking automobile, it will sell for about $100 more than roadster.

The new three-cylinder engine replaces earlier two-cylinder job. Three carburetors are used.

SPECIFICATIONS

Maker: Berkeley Coachwork, Ltd., Biggleswade, Bedfordshire, England
Cylinders: Three (two-stroke engine), front-wheel drive
Bore: 58 mm.
Stroke: 62 mm.
Capacity: 492 cc.
Compression ratio: 7.4 to 1
Valves: None
Cooling: Air
Maximum horsepower: 30 at 5,500 r.p.m.
Gearshift: On steering column
Speeds: Three
Final drive: Open chain
Steering: Burman worm and nut
Suspension front: Coil springs
          rear: Coil springs
Brakes: Girling, 7 in. diameter, total lining area 65 sq. in.
Tires: 5.20 x 12
Battery: 12 volt
Seats: Two
Doors: Two
Weight: 725 lbs.
Wheelbase: 70 in.
Length overall: 122.5 in.
Width overall: 50 in.
Height overall: 43.5 in.
Instruments: Speedometer, fuel gauge, ammeter
Turning circle: 28 feet
Ground clearance: 5 in.
Price: $1,745 (coupe $1,850)

Berkeley Sports

ar makes NEWS!

The Berkeley has astonished the public, followers of Motor Sport and the Motoring Press by its amazing performances in racing, rallies and driving tests.

B.A.R.C. MEETING AT GOODWOOD, JUNE 10.

Autosport (June 14, 1957).

"The tiny red Berkeley, driven by Goddard-Watts, cheekily challenged a MK VII Jaguar and set up a new 350 lap record at 58.02 m.p.h."

Autocar (June 14, 1957).

"The spectacle of J. Goddard-Watts in a Berkeley catching and trying to pass I. M. Gillet's MK VII Jaguar is not one that will quickly be forgotten."

B.A.R.C. MEETING AT AINTREE, JUNE 15.

Autocar (June 21, 1957).

"All eyes were on the trim little vermilion Berkeley in handicap 'A,' and sure enough it won. The winning speed of 53.25 m.p.h. should not be overlooked. From 328 c.c. this is not bad going."

BRIGHTON MOTOR RALLY, JUNE 22.

Brighton Evening Argus (June 24, 1957).

"I. Mantle was driving one of the four smallest cars in the event—a 328 c.c. two-stroke Berkeley sports. He won his class. His Berkeley showed what it was made of when it lifted its nearside rear wheel under the stresses of acceleration and fast cornering."

B.R.S.C.C. MEETING AT BRANDS HATCH, AUGUST 5.

Autocar (*August* 9, 1957).

"A swarm of 328 c.c. 2-stroke Berkeleys hummed around for ten laps, after a Le Mans-type start. Impressive, stable, they showed a fair turn of speed as the winner's average of 55.25 m.p.h. confirms."

Autosport (*August* 9, 1957).

"A ten lap race for Berkeley sports cars produced 14 of these little machines, which buzzed round at surprisingly high speeds for 328 c.c. Goddard-Watts gradually outstripped his rivals, lapping at over 57 m.p.h. in the process."

SILVERSTONE CLUB RACING, SEPTEMBER 27.

Autosport (*October* 4, 1957) *commenting on the 1½ litre race, says:*

"The first (race) was notable for the quite incredible speed exhibited by Graham's little red Berkeley. Its first challenge came from D. Rees in his Austin Special, but he disappeared and Arthur Mallock arrived in a hurry to take his place, but the Berkeley managed to keep on its tail for a whole lap after being passed, although one would not have thought that the Club circuit at Silverstone was ideally suited to this miniature projectile."

BERKELEY   CARS   LIMITED   BIGGLESWADE   BEDS

ROAD TEST BERKELEY

PEOPLE DO LAUGH at the Berkeley—that is, those who haven't driven it. As these heart-warming little sports cars become more numerous here, you may see their drivers laughing, too. We did, and from the fun of it. For this minute combination of utter overall economy with driving enjoyment is the result of an ingenious approach to simplification that rivals that of the Citroen 2-CV.

The car is so small that it seems impossible for a large driver even to get in, much less drive in comfort. The latter is by far the easier, particularly when the Berkeley is parked by a curb, with which the seat is likely to be approximately level. Once inside, conditions improve. There is lots of foot room around the pedals and on the seat, though shoulders are cramped with a passenger aboard. The windshield is adequately high. The seat, covered with plastic, is suspended on broad rubber strips from a tube frame. For more or less distance from the pedals and wheel, the strips can be loosened or tightened. A fuel gauge

and ammeter will likely be added to the austere panel on later cars.

The only checking-out needed for the first-time Berkeley driver is on the motorcycle-style progressive gearbox. An improvement over the prototype's column-mounted shift, the lever is now on the floor. Reverse, 1st, main neutral, 2nd and 3rd are in a more-or-less straight line from front to rear; gates give the clue to the different gears. Additional neutral positions appear between all gears. A mere flick shoots the lever from 2nd to high and back; reverse and low are not so easy to engage with certainty, but one soon comes to depend on a tiny clunk (felt rather than heard) to indicate engagement. The clutch is soft but sudden.

A pleasant surprise comes with a push on the starter button, for the Siba Dynastart—a combined starter/generator, as the name indicates—sets the 2-stroke engine in motion with total silence and no delay. A motorcycle-type choke is under the

PHOTOGRAPHY: POOLE

"What a curious feeling!" said Alice. "I must be shutting up like a telescope."

dash, but hardly needed. A great willingness to rev up and the characteristic smoothness of a 2 stroke make acceleration a pleasure and the 20-cubic-inch displacement even less probable. The acceleration figures at right, though they cannot compare with those for big cars, give no indication of the feeling while driving. A loud exhaust and the low seat tend to cancel out the objective evidence of the speedometer.

Decelerating and idling produce sputtering and popping that can irritate the sensitive. Though we continued to be aware of them, they did not bother us after the first few minutes.

Steering the Berkeley is pure delight. Though the front wheels support nearly 70% of the total weight, that portion amounts to all of 500 pounds. Accelerating through a corner will counteract the fly-away feeling of the light rear end and convert it to tractable understeer. When pressed beyond prudent limits on slippery roads, the front end will be the first to wash out.

The high-quality plastic structure, reinforced with aluminum, results in a staunchness untroubled by rattles or a weaving cowl. A non-leaning and generally non-bottoming ride is remarkably comfortable on most surfaces, but caution is advisable to avoid holes in the pavement, into which the 12-inch wheels can drop most unnervingly. Really rough roads, too, are not the forte of any 70-inch-wheelbase car.

Girling combination shock absorber and coil spring units are used with the swing axles at the rear and the wishbones at the front. A closed chain connects the crankshaft to the gearbox, which sits behind the air-cooled engine; from the gearbox an open chain goes to the differential. The usual erratic front-drive cornering is present at slow speeds only.

Dual Amal carburetors may be expected on later models. Our test car had only one, but of course had the 8.20:1 compression ratio that is optional in fuel-conscious England. A trouble-free touch is the gravity feed fuel tank (the mixture is a quart of oil to 4 gallons of gas). A desirable improvement, especially until a fuel gauge becomes standard, would be tipping the tank to make the last ¾ inch more predictably usable.

Far more than adequate 7-inch brakes with a total lining area of 65 square inches, and a surprising variety and amount of package space complete this package of piquant practicality.

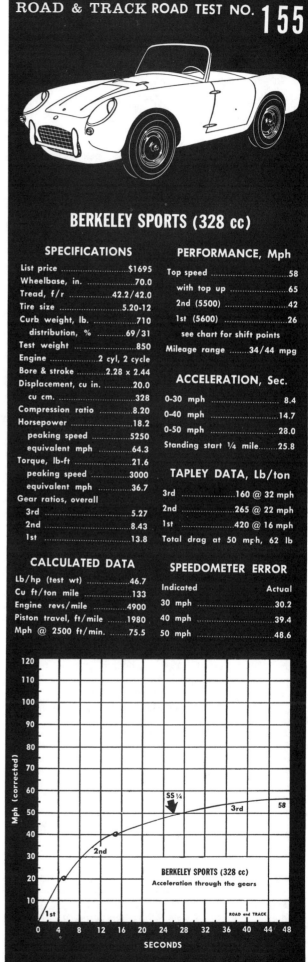

BERKELEY SPORTS (328 cc)

SPECIFICATIONS

List price	$1695
Wheelbase, in.	70.0
Tread, f/r	42.2/42.0
Tire size	5.20-12
Curb weight, lb.	710
distribution, %	69/31
Test weight	850
Engine	2 cyl, 2 cycle
Bore & stroke	2.28 x 2.44
Displacement, cu in.	20.0
cu cm.	328
Compression ratio	8.20
Horsepower	18.2
peaking speed	5250
equivalent mph	64.3
Torque, lb-ft	21.6
peaking speed	3000
equivalent mph	36.7
Gear ratios, overall	
3rd	5.27
2nd	8.43
1st	13.8

PERFORMANCE, Mph

Top speed	58
with top up	65
2nd (5500)	42
1st (5600)	26
see chart for shift points	
Mileage range	34/44 mpg

ACCELERATION, Sec.

0-30 mph	8.4
0-40 mph	14.7
0-50 mph	28.0
Standing start ¼ mile	25.8

TAPLEY DATA, Lb/ton

3rd	160 @ 32 mph
2nd	265 @ 22 mph
1st	420 @ 16 mph
Total drag at 50 mph, 62 lb	

CALCULATED DATA

Lb/hp (test wt)	46.7
Cu ft/ton mile	133
Engine revs/mile	4900
Piston travel, ft/mile	1980
Mph @ 2500 ft/min.	75.5

SPEEDOMETER ERROR

Indicated	Actual
30 mph	30.2
40 mph	39.4
50 mph	48.6

BERKELEY SPORTS (328 cc)
Acceleration through the gears

ROAD and TRACK

If the front-wheel Berkeley is "pulled" around the corners, it behaves like it's part of the road. Because of its low power (top speed about 60 mph), it is extremely difficult to develop—and hold—large slip angles ,or to get into trouble.

THE Berkeley Sports is a small but very sociable car. From the moment we pulled out of the Berkeley garage we began to make new friends. And the car is definitely an attention getter.

Driving out into New York's garment-district traffic, we braked to a halt behind a huge tractor-trailer. Immediately another pulled up behind, and a third came out of a driveway, stopping with his bumper nuzzling the right door: sort of like being dropped in the middle of a herd of Brontosaurii. The driver of the truck behind stepped out and said "Small, ain't it? I bet I can pick that thing up." And he did! But he was quite surprised when we slipped the car into gear and eased it ahead, forcing him to run along with his hands full of car, like a reluctant barrow-pusher.

The Berkeley at this point had only twenty-seven miles on the odometer. In all conscience it was impossible to conduct a road test until at least two thousand miles were on the clock, so the car was run for four days before it was put under the stop watch and subjected to the scrutiny of the SCI staff. Fortunately, these four days represented a variety of conditions: a summer-like day; a rainy day; a day that was cold; and the last day, in which we conducted the performance testing, was cold, sun-less and dry.

The first thing we did was lift the hood, wherein dwells the Excelsior "Talisman Twin" vertical two-stroke engine with a *full* 328 cc pumping a *full* 18 horses. The two KLG sparkplugs are connected to two coils, with a set of points for each plug. There is no sump since the engine is lubricated by the petroil system, which mixes one part lube oil to sixteen parts gasoline (one quart to four gallons). In appearance the engine looks as though it was originally de-

Two-stroke two-cylinder 328 cc engine has 1 plug, 1 coil and 1 carb per cylinder. Fuel tank, foreground. At right is Siba Dynastart, combination starter-generator.

Instruments include speedometer calibrated to 120 mph, fuel gauge, ammeter. Reinforcing struts at edges of windshield are very practical. Gate-type gear shift splits cockpit. Jump seat/storage compartment deck pivots upward from seatback.

Storage shelf under dash is very large, and there is no tunnel. Progressive gear shift pattern moves aft through two neutrals.

Jump seat will hold small child, but an adult will not fit in. Removing back of jump seat reveals huge storage compartment, holds roof. If edges are trimmed, spare will fit in, too.

signed for a motorcycle—perhaps because it was.

On a cold day the engine is not an immediate starter. The owner's manual prescribes that the choke should be fully closed, the throttle about half open (or half closed) and the engine cranked. It worked, but it took a few turns. It's a consolation to look at the full-size battery, then the size of the engine with its built-up roller-bearing crank, and realize the number of turns one has before exhausting the charge. The starter is small; it will not move the car on the battery. On the other hand, once the engine is up to temperature, the starting is literally push-button. The slightest touch fires the engine up with absolutely no starter noise. It saves a lot of embarrassment for the driver who is prone toward stalling, as one might be until he learns he has to scream the engine out before easing the clutch. The starting motor is the Siba Dynastart, which combines the functions of cranking the engine and charging the battery in a single unit. It's a handy way to save space and weight.

Once running, the engine is uneven, as may be expected from a two-stroke unit with the engine exhausting towards the ground under the belly pan. A great deal of the exhaust noise reverberates into the cockpit. Once on the road, however, the story changes. First gear gives you a definite feel of acceleration, for the engine winds up quickly. Top is about 20 in first; then to second, where the Berkeley is less snappy up to about 35. This is the point to shift the compromise between engine noise and acceleration. From here the car pulls all the way up to 60. The most comfortable cruising speed is between 50 and 55. The engine produces enough power at this rpm to level out road rises and there is very little vibration. If you get caught with your revs down on

We forced the Berkeley sideways by cutting wheel, hitting brakes; no matter how rough we were, wheel correction and power brought tail in line. We were never in serious trouble.

most any hill, you have to be a man of patience. You can only get so much power from less than a third of a liter, but our test car, not yet fully broken in and at no time driven as if we were on an economy run, gave us an honest *57 miles per gallon of fuel*. The engine just can't burn enough fuel to get the half-ton of car and passengers up the hills in a hurry.

The clutch operates smoothly and easily and the gears can be changed without using the entire clutch throw. It is, however, what used to be called a "suicide" clutch—all of a sudden you've got it. Once you know it's there, though, you soon get used to it and get to like it. It's a multiple disc unit that really bites.

A progressive-pattern remote-linkage crash-transmission ties the engine to the driving front axle. There is really no shift pattern; to engage first gear from neutral merely pull the shift lever one notch toward you, until you hit a stop. To engage second, move the lever off the stop and pull until you hit another stop. Third gear is engaged by moving off the second stop and pulling down to the bottom of the gate. That's all there is—there are only three forward speeds. Fourth was converted to reverse, and is engaged by working up through the pattern as far forward as you can go. Incidentally, there are *three* neutrals—one between each cog. It's a very convenient fool-proof shift that is a cinch to manipulate once you get used to it.

To say adequate for the brakes would be to sell them short. A car that weighs 760 pounds dry needs far less than the Berkeley's allotted 65 square inches of lining to be described as adequately braked. This is 171 inches of lining per ton dry. Wet, with passengers, the ratio is closer to 125 square inches per ton; the stopping power is excellent. At low speed, up to maybe 40 mph, the slightest touch on the pedal with the tow of the shoe brings the car to a fast, gentle stop. At high speed (50 to 60 mph) only slightly more pressure is needed. This is to be expected when one considers two factors: the brakes are oversize, probably designed for a larger car; the heat energy dissipation factor of the linings is greater than the kinetic energy developing capacity of the engine (remember that 57 mpg). On our very punishing brake test there was no sign of fade. The light-weight rear however, does present a problem: it doesn't take too much push on the pedal to lock up the rear wheels, and if you push too hard with the front wheels cocked, you'll find yourself sideways.

The brakes are good but stopping can be tricky. To see just how tricky, we took the car on a winding Connecticut road and tried to bend it. We sneaked up on a curve at 55 mph, cut the wheel sharply to the right, and slammed on the brakes. Immediately the tail swung way out to the left, and a lot more steering correction was needed than one normally expects. There just isn't enough weight on the rear to keep it stable, and the front wheels do most of the stopping. The rear lifts and tries to catch up with the front end. The car slides, however, and we do not believe that a driver of fair ability could get the car to go fast enough to get himself into any trouble that he couldn't get out of. We whipped it for all it had, contorted it, and never felt as if we were really going to lose it.

There's only one way to describe the steering—quick. With 2¼ turns lock to lock, it doesn't take much wheel motion to get around bends and curves. Steering is extremely fast, and there doesn't appear to be very much wheel return. You have to turn it in and then turn it out of the curves—usually requiring no more than a half-turn. Yet on extremely rough and choppy roads very little shock is transmitted back to the driver through the wheel. One thing, however, can be felt.

The power is transmitted through a pair of Hardy-Spicer joints that do not transmit constant-velocity. On straights it's not noticeable; but you can feel it on the turns. It's particularly bad—you can feel the power surges—when starting from a dead stop in full lock, as in the case of making a U-turn. The wear factor is likely to be quite high.

But once in motion it's easy to forgive these minor faults. The car tracks well on the straight and requires little attention. There is very little urge to wander, but turning may feel a bit strange to the driver accustomed to rear-wheel drive. The front drive, coupled with the lightweight rear, requires getting used to.

One of the sit-down-first-then-put-the-legs-in variety. Berkeley has a good finish, plenty of glass area, and independent rear suspension.

The Associate Editor parked by pulling abreast of a space, bouncing in front, and walking in the rear.

Seven inch brake drum is more than adequate for 760 pound car. Chrome hub is slitted for cooling air, and is held on by knock-off hub.

Wishbone front end with Girling coil spring and shock unit. Torque is transmitted through Hardy-Spicer joint.

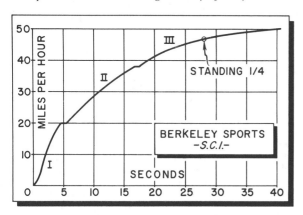

Tension-adjustable rubber spanners are base for seat pad, which is surprisingly comfortable.

BERKELEY SPORTS

TEST CONDITIONS:

Number aboard	2
Top position	up
Temperature	50°
Etc.	full fuel tank, weather clear

PERFORMANCE

TOP SPEED:

Two-way average	59 mph
Fastest one-way run	60.5 mph

ACCELERATION:

From zero to

20 mph	4.6 sec
30 mph	11.0 sec
40 mph	18.9 sec
50 mph	39.1 sec
Standing ¼ mile	27.9 sec
Speed at end of quarter	46.4 mph

SPEED RANGES IN GEARS:

I	0-18 mph
II	15-40 mph
III	25-top

SPEEDOMETER CORRECTION:

Indicated	Actual
20	19 mph
30	28 mph
40	38 mph
50	47 mph
60	55 mph

FUEL CONSUMPTION:

Average driving (45-60 mph)	57 mpg

BRAKING EFFICIENCY (10 successive emergency stops from 40 mph, just short of locking wheels):

1st stop	50
2nd	50
3rd	58
4th	62
5th	65
6th	65
7th	65
8th	65
9th	65
10th stop	65

Note: Pedal High, No Fade.

SPECIFICATIONS

POWER UNIT:

Type	Vertical Twin, two-stroke
Valve Arrangement	None (cylinder wall ports)
Bore & Stroke	2.28 x 2.44 in (58 x 62 mm)
Stroke/Bore Ratio	1.07/1
Displacement	20 cu in (328 cc)
Compression Ratio	7.9:1
Carburetion by	Twin Amals
Max. power	18 hp @ 5000 rpm

DRIVE TRAIN:

Transmission ratios:

I	13.85
II	8.34
III	5.27
Final drive by open chain	
Axle torque taken by	wishbone

CHASSIS:

Wheelbase	70 in
Front Tread	42.25 in
Rear Tread	42 in
Suspension, front	Independent, wishbone, coil spring
Suspension, rear	Independet, swing axle, coil spring
Shock absorbers	Girling
Steering type	Burman worm and nut
Steering wheel turns L to L	2.25
Turning diameter	28 ft.
Brake type	Girling Hydraulic
Brake lining area	65 sq. in.
Tire size	5.20 x 12

GENERAL:

Length	130 in
Height	42 in
Weight, test car	760 pounds
Weight distribution, F/R	34/66
Weight distribution, F/R, with driver	41/59
Fuel capacity	3.6 U. S. gal.

RATING FACTORS:

Bhp per cu. in.	0.90
Bhp per sq. in. piston area	2.20
Pounds per bhp—test car	42.2 dry; 55.5 with passengers
Piston speed @ max bhp	2040 fpm
Brake lining area per ton	171 sq. in. dry; 130 sq. in. with passengers

At low speeds, say up to 35 mph, and no matter how gently the wheel is turned for a curve, there is an immediate necessity to cut back to correct. Not dangerous, but it's there. But as velocity increases, the feeling is less acute, until at about 50 mph the condition disappears. Steering becomes effortless.

There is not enough engine and not enough speed to get into a drift. Besides, it feels a lot more comfortable when you're *pulling* around the corner. There is very little lean, and what there is, is unnoticeable from the cockpit. It gives the driver a lot of confidence.

The ride is exceptionally good for a car with only 70 inches of wheelbase: small bumps are absorbed by the suspension and never get to the "frame". No pitching was noticeable, and the shock absorbers must certainly be very much oversize. They work well, and it takes a choppy washboard condition to make you aware that you are not cruising on a new turnpike.

The car is small, and this quality is more than apparent when entering and exiting. It's one of the sit-down-first-then-put-the-legs-in type. If you're average in height you can do it easily; if tall, you'd better be agile. Once in, however, you're in for a pleasant surprise.

The seat appears to be nothing more than a mat spread over the floor. Examination showed that it was actually a soft, padded mat suspended on rubber impact-absorbing adjustable-tension straps. The one-piece cushion is anchored by tap screws on the sides, and these hold it securely. It is surprisingly comfortable despite the lack of fore-and-aft adjustment.

The seats have no bucket-affect whatsoever, but you don't seem to miss it. When driving alone, the driver knows what he's going to do and braces himself; with a passenger, the two occupants support each other very firmly. With the roof up two people are a snug but comfortable fit; with the roof down, we carried two passengers a pretty fair distance without interfering with the operation of the car or seriously discommoding the passengers. The absence of a tunnel provides a lot more passenger space than might be at first supposed, but over the winter months its not a good idea to ride with someone you don't like.

The roof is good-quality rubberized canvas that can be erected quickly and easily. A rolled insulation bond is sewed on to every edge all the way around, sealing off any drafts. The sidecurtains just drop in and pop out, secured in place by a single snap fastener that secures the vent slit (inadvertently we once closed both doors with these snaps fastened on both sides, and had to solicit the aid of a passing youngster, whose arm was small enough to squeeze between the top and the curtain). However, the abundance of glass area (clear vinyl) cut into the top and the design of the curtains provide about 320 degree visibility. The remaining 40 degrees of blind spot are located where visibility is least needed—the area the driver can see by merely turning his head.

The steering wheel is located close to the dash panel. It is a position comfortable for most any driver, but long legs seemed to have difficulty clearing the edge of the wheel. However, this did not interfere with control. Foot pedals are the conventional clutch, brake and accelerator located in the conventional places. Since there is no adjustment on the seat, one either fits or one doesn't. There is no middle ground. The car needs a foot rest next to the accelerator; over a long stretch the throttle foot had a tendency to "go to sleep".

The instruments include a speedometer (calibrated to 120 mph!), an ammeter and a fuel gauge. Apparently the manufacturer feels there is no need for a temperature gauge on an engine that is awfully difficult to overheat, and there is no oil under pressure. All are well placed, readable, and well illuminated at night, without the fault of blinding the driver, and the instrument lights can be turned off by a separate switch if the driver desires. The small controls are well placed, too. They are unmarked, but there are only three of them—running lights, dash light switch and electric wipers. The choke is under the dash but it's easy to locate and operate. The handbrake locks the rear wheels with very little pull, and is located to the left of the driver and out of the way.

Storage space, because of the physical size of the car, seems inadequate; yet really there is plenty. Inside the cockpit, the entire underside of the dash is one big shelf, large enough to carry all kinds of assorted gear and even large enough for small cases. Cigarettes, scarves, gloves *et al* can be carried in the sizable door pockets.

The entire rear of the car, running from the seat backrest to the bumper, is all available for storage space, occupied only by the spare wheel. After turning the two Dzus keys that lock the trunk, the cover hinges forward, exposing a jump seat suitable for one small child. An adult cannot physically fit into it. Either of the two spring-loaded snaps may be pushed, completely detaching the lid. The spare wheel is stored where the legs would normally be located if the jump seat were used.

The release of another Dzus at the rear of the jump compartment removes another panel and exposes a cavernous space where the top, tonneau cover and tool set is stored. We noticed that by merely trimming away a bit on the fiberglass at the edges, it would be possible to store the spare in here, too. This makes the entire jump seat space available as more readily accessible luggage storage. And with the top up this section can be left permanently, making access a lot easier. Since this section hinges from the front, it is necessary to unsnap the roof to put anything in or take anything out.

The "frame" is set inside the beautifully-finished fibreglass, giving a full belly-pan effect, except that the body is cast as a one-piece unit. With the top up the sealing is perfect, except for minor drafts entering through gaps in the side curtains. Even in a driving rain, our car remained dry.

To erect the top, it is necessary to assemble the cross piece, which is composed of two half-sections joined at the center by a male-female joint. The roof snaps align well, and the whole operation can be done a lot quicker than it would take to read the directions on how to do it.

And it is much the same with maintaining the car. After twisting a single Dzus, the hood is held up by a rod that locks in a slot. The spark plugs are there where you can get at them. The battery, master cylinder, ignition coils, wiring, carburetors, fuel tank, drive chain, and everything that is serviced can be reached from above—easily. And all the running components—steering gear, universal joints, etc.—are accessible from the aft side of each front wheel. A screwdriver, pliers, and a two dollar grease gun puts you in your own maintenance business, and you could do most of the jobs dressed in a tuxedo. It's as simple as that.

Another feature that impressed us was the efficiency of the headlights. Incidentally, the headlights on our car look as though they were dropped on the fenders as an afterthought; actually they were. On non-export British models, the headlight is faired into the fender; in this country several states have refused to pass this faired-in headlight on their safety inspections. However, Tony Pompeo assures us that you can order your Berkeley with the headlights faired-in, if you wish, and take your chances on inspections. Any way you take it, the bulb is a real, honest-to-goodness twelve-volt *sealed beam*.

There is no provision for a heater in the car, and it would be difficult to mount one. Without heat, the car cannot honestly be called all-weather transportation. Considering its displacement it's quite lively, although another 172 cc would not be unwelcome, especially on the hills. But these faults are balanced by the solid, beautifully-finished body with every snap and clamp placed in exactly the right spot. It's truly a fun-car on an economy budget —the total cost of ownership has to be low —and there's one thing for sure: you'll save money on parking meters!

Len Griffing

The Berkeley structure is almost entirely of glass fibre. The bonnet lid is hinged at the front. "Over-riders" provide firm protection

Berkeley 492 c.c. Sports
DE LUXE

STILL very new to the motor industry, the name of Berkeley is becoming increasingly widely known as the production line at Biggleswade in Bedfordshire—now producing on average about 50 cars per week—gets into its stride. At race meetings, special events even have been programmed for the make—mostly for the little two-cylinder 328 c.c. version, of which a test was published in *The Autocar* dated 10 January, 1958.

The three-cylinder model which is the subject of the present test was introduced at the 1957 London Motor Show, and is powered by a 492 c.c. air-cooled two-stroke Excelsior engine, for which an output of 30 b.h.p. (gross) is claimed; the results achieved certainly substantiate this figure. Thus the Berkeley has progressed into an entirely different performance category, and the three-cylinder model can be termed a true sports car.

For those unfamiliar with the make, the Berkeley is constructed almost entirely of glass-reinforced polyester resin, the three main mouldings—a punt-shaped base, the bonnet and tail—being bolted together to form a unit which does not depend upon a separate chassis frame. Engine and transmission are supported by a steel sub-frame, however, and there is also an aluminium alloy bulkhead. This construction makes for exceptionally light weight, the test car, with a full tank (5 gallons) and ready for the road, scaling only 7.5 cwt.

The three-cylinder engine has the same cylinder dimensions as the twin (58mm bore, 62mm stroke), is of the transfer-port type, and is fed by a separate Amal Monobloc carburettor to each cylinder. It is mounted transversely, forward of the front wheel centres. At one end of the crankcase is a Siba Dynastart, which is used for starting and as a generator for the battery, and also incorporates a low-tension make-and-break assembly to feed three individual coils.

At the other end of the crankshaft, a double-roller primary chain carries the drive to a motor-cycle-type multi-plate clutch running in oil, and thence to an Albion four-speed quadrant change gear box (incorporating also a reverse) which is bolted to the back face of the crankcase below the carburettor. An open roller chain transmits the drive thence to a chassis-mounted differential, the front hubs being carried on wishbones of unequal length, and the wheels driven by universally jointed shafts. The rear wheels are also carried independently on swing axles, while Girling coil spring-and-damper units are used for all four wheels.

Particularly while the car is a novelty to them, drivers will tend to use the gears and high r.p.m. freely, and hence increase the fuel consumption. This fact, and the performance testing also included, no doubt account for our rather low overall m.p.g. figure. There should be no difficulty in obtaining well over 40 m.p.g. for out-of-town journeys.

It is surely a remarkable achievement that this baby car should record a mean maximum speed of 80 m.p.h.; this has not been attained by freak gearing, since acceleration figures are thoroughly in keeping. For instance, to reach 50 m.p.h. in 14.4sec is no mean feat, and the standing-start quarter-mile figure of 22.4sec, whereby it can show a clean pair of heels to some family saloons with engines up to five times the size, is also highly creditable.

These figures are partly owed to especially suitable spacing of the gear ratios, giving maxima in increments of approximately 20 m.p.h. between first and second and between second and third, the last-named ratio peaking at 70 m.p.h. In fact, the useful range of third gear extends from about 25 m.p.h. up to its maximum, so that it can be used fre-

Ease of entry and exit is unusually good for such a small sports car. The instruments, lettered in white on black, are (from left to right) rev counter, ammeter, fuel gauge, and speedometer with total and trip mileage recorders. On the right of the facia is the screen washer control. When not in use the hood is stowed in the lidded compartment between the seats and the luggage grid

Separate amber winking indicators are fitted beneath the recessed head lamps, which incorporate parking lights. From certain angles the tidy appearance is marred by the protrusion of the ornate wheel trims, which can easily strike a high kerb. If the spare wheel is mounted on the luggage rack, additional interior space is provided for baggage; normally the wheel is stowed immediately behind the seats or under the scuttle

Berkeley 492 c.c. Sports . . .

quently in traffic at one end of the scale, and provide close support to top gear at the other.

The power unit produced an exhilarating noise, more closely comparable with that of a Grand Prix car than with a touring road vehicle. The exhaust note is unnecessarily obtrusive and attracts unwelcome attention, especially at the high revs which are required to get the best performance. At low revs and on part throttle, the engine spent much of its time burbling unevenly, and would fire on every stroke only when pulling. Throughout a rather wide intermediate range, there was considerable high-frequency vibration which transmitted itself through the steering-column to the driver's hands, but at its highest crankshaft speeds, the unit became again extremely smooth up to the maker's recommended limit of 6,500 r.p.m.

A 16 to 1 mixture of petrol and oil (two gallons to a pint) is specified—a rather extravagant diet in contrast with continental water-cooled two-strokes, which now are operating on mixture ratios of up to 40 to 1.

At first acquaintance, the lightning speed with which engine revs will build up—indeed, it is all too easy to send the revolution counter needle rushing well beyond the graduated scale, especially if a gear is missed—and the accompanying spirited uproar are rather rewarding, but once the novelty has worn thin, one pines for less fuss and noise. It would appear that the carburettors are difficult to seal against fuel leakage, and there was a pronounced smell of petrol in the cockpit throughout most of the testing.

The combination of very haphazard idling and an insen-

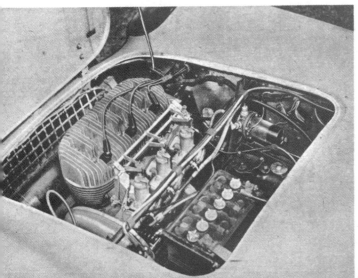

The three-cylinder Excelsior engine is mounted just behind the radiator grille, each cylinder having its own carburettor. Battery and fuel pump are easily reached. Part of the chain drive to the differential can be seen beside the clutch housing, under the nearest carburettor

sitive and fierce clutch, of which the pedal could be released only in jerks due to friction in the operating cable, made take-offs from rest most difficult in the extreme. Even after considerable acquaintance with the car, it was all too easy to stall the engine whilst trying to get away; a consolation was that the Siba Dynastart enabled one to re-start the engine instantly at the pressure of a button on the facia. Once on the move, the clutch did all that was asked of it, and showed no tendency to slip during repeated gear changes; it was found impossible, however, to re-start the Berkeley on a one-in-four gradient without overtaxing the clutch; during our attempts there was also some difficulty with front-wheel spin. There was never a sign of clutch drag.

In the absence of winter conditions we were unable to establish whether the dynamo-small-battery combination would be adequate to meet all demands, but several starts in the period of an hour's run, when head lamps and wipers were also in use, left the battery noticeably flat.

Considerable improvement has been made in the gear-change mechanism since the first Berkeleys were produced, and the lever motion in its selector quadrant is very reasonably definite. It was often impossible to engage first or reverse gears from a standstill without first releasing the clutch to spin the gear pinions a little. The gear change mechanism is light; indeed, with the pressure of one or two fingers only behind the lever, the driver is less likely to overshoot one ratio and pass into the next. The quadrant lever, mounted centrally on the floor, is arranged to engage reverse when pushed fully forward, and is pulled back towards the driver for neutral and the four forward ratios. The lever is spring-loaded to the right; to engage second, it must first be sprung left before bringing it back. For the other two upward changes, the spring loading resets the lever after each engagement, so that only a straight pull back is called for.

When changing down, top to third is a direct movement, but the lever has to be pressed to the left when changing from third to second and second to first. The constant-mesh gears are engaged by dogs, but double-declutching is not called for, and the change demands little skill of the driver. Uneven firing of the engine at low crankshaft revolutions accentuates the lack of spring in the transmission—always a feature of cars having their power units adjacent to the final drive, without the torsional resilience of a long propeller-shaft to absorb shock.

Moreover, since the drive shaft universal joints are not of the constant-velocity type, on very sharp turns there is some front-wheel flap which comes back to the driver's hands. Since its comparatively recent introduction the Berkeley has earned an excellent reputation for general roadworthiness, in terms of cornering powers, steering and brakes, but these qualities require further qualification.

The combination of front wheel drive, a low centre of gravity, and a comparatively wide track result in a high standard of stability on wet and dry roads. The car gives a very satisfactory ride for its occupants considering its

42

 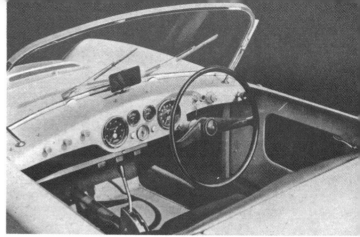

There is luggage space behind the seats which may be covered by the glass fibre panel seen in place on the right. The horn button, matching the starter control, is placed to the left of the clock, an optional extra. The gear lever operates in a fore-and-aft quadrant, with notches in the "gate" to assist positive location of each gear position

Lilliputian dimensions, and normally its cornering abilities are extremely high, nor is there any apparent tendency to roll. On the other hand, certain steering characteristics make it a little treacherous at times, particularly when the throttle is not wide open. There is no caster action of the front wheels, and some artificial centring means, such as the incorporation of centralizing springs in the rack-and-pinion steering gear, would be appreciated by drivers accustomed to more conventional vehicles.

Whilst the engine is pulling the Berkeley can be aimed precisely and pleasantly, but on the overrun or on very light throttle loads, the steering becomes somewhat dead, and over rough surfaces there is a tendency to wander. Normally, this reduction in directional stability never embarrasses except while braking from high speed, or when cornering on a rough surface, whereupon a slight alteration in power applied will change its characteristics. When, for example, a roundabout is taken fast, there is some tendency for the front to dig into the corner.

The steering requires a little more work than expected at low speeds, and over uneven ground there is considerable vertical shake of the column.

It will be seen from the performance tables that excellent braking figures were achieved, as with the previous Berkeley tested. Under full power braking, some right lock had to be applied to keep the car on a straight course, nor were the brakes completely smooth in operation. The subsequent failure of a brake drum suggests that this may have been due to some misalignment or eccentricity of that particular drum. Pedal pressures were always reasonably light, and the brakes proved able to withstand hard driving tactics without fade. The umbrella-handle-type hand-brake beneath the facia on the driver's right was found to be fully able to hold the laden car on a one-in-three gradient.

Development work on the body has included the lengthening of the doors by 5in, so that the current Berkeley is much easier to enter and leave than the earliest models. Moreover the seating, with plastic trim over shaped foam-rubber cushions, has been much improved, while at the same time there has been an increase in leg room. A tall driver, however, may well find that the accelerator pedal is a little close, but without the luxury of a seating adjustment, a compromise position, of course, has had to be chosen.

The steering-wheel is too close to the driver for comfort or to allow the currently fashionable arms-outstretched driving position, and the internal width of the car is such that the driver with passenger may find some slight restriction on elbow movements. Since the wheel rim has several inches of clearance from the facia panel, there would seem to be no obvious difficulty in fitting a shorter steering column.

A well-equipped facia panel includes, in the centre, a most necessary revolution counter peaking at 7,000 r.p.m., an almost accurate speedometer, which incorporates total and trip distance recorders, an electric clock, ammeter and fuel contents gauge. Also in the centre are identical push-buttons for the horn and self-starter; it would be more convenient in an emergency if the horn button was either in the steering wheel boss, or beside the screen-washer plunger to the extreme right of the driver.

Flashing signal lamps are operated by a switch, which is not self-cancelling, in front of the driver, and the lamps, screen wipers and instrument panel lights are controlled by three push-pull switches in front of the passenger. The screen wipers are not self-parking, and their blades could be extended by nearly 2in to cover a much larger area of the curved screen. Beneath the facia are deep shelves, of which the one on the left can be used to carry the spare wheel when the rear compartment is required for other purposes; the folded tonneau cover will stow away neatly in the right-hand compartment.

In addition, there are large apertures in the doors for stowing maps and other oddments. The rear-view mirror, mounted on the scuttle just behind the lower windscreen frame, is too low to reflect much more than the driver's and passenger's shoulders, and a suction-type mirror higher up on the windscreen itself would be more effective.

An adequate beam was given by the faired-in head lamps, but some of their illumination was visible through the extractor slot in the bonnet top, and proved distracting for the driver. Since the left foot is already very fully employed with frequent gear-changing, a manual dip-switch would be preferable. Rough-weather equipment includes a

In spite of the diminutive appearance of the car on the road, two grown-ups, a child and luggage can all be carried internally without squeezing them in

Berkeley 492 c.c. Sports...

plastic hood, of which the front edge knuckles round a lip on the top rail of the windscreen frame—a somewhat unorthodox attachment which proved fully effective in practice. It is supported by a light tubular frame, in interlocking halves, which drops into plated metal sockets just behind the seat squab. It appeared that the Lift-a-Dot fasteners by which the back of the hood is secured to the rear panel are scarcely adequate for the job; a more substantial type of fastener would deal with the hood in cold weather, when the plastic material is not so supple and easy to stretch.

Large side screens (the frames of which drop into sockets in the doors) give excellent protection and allow good vision. The panels are of flexible plastic and incorporate a free flap for signalling and for reaching the door handles from outside. It was found, however, that with the hood and side screens in position, there was insufficient ventilation, and some fresh-air inlet would be greatly appreciated during summer showers.

Behind the passenger's seat is a removable panel secured by a carriage key, and beneath this is space either for a little luggage, or if the spare wheel and hood frames are removed and placed beneath the facia, two small children could sit here safely. Behind this is a further luggage space in the tail of the car, reached through a second, flexible panel. Moreover, on the car tested there was a chromed luggage rack mounted over the tail panel, to which the spare wheel could be attached in preference to luggage which could then remain clean and dry inside.

Cheapest and smallest of British sports cars, and certainly of most original and enterprising design, the Berkeley is quite unexpectedly agile, dimensionally handy for city traffic (although insufficiently tractable), generally comfortable and weather-tight. And, incidentally, it should attract motor-cyclists who wish to graduate one step upwards from a side-car outfit, and who may well be on familiar terms with air-cooled two-strokes and part-chain transmission.

BERKELEY 492 c.c. SPORTS DE LUXE

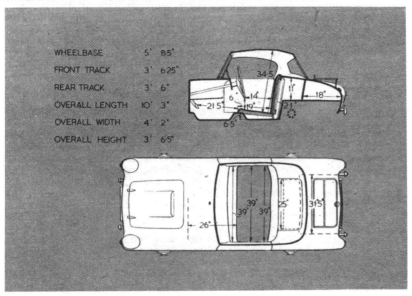

WHEELBASE	5' 8·5"	
FRONT TRACK	3' 6·25"	
REAR TRACK	3' 6"	
OVERALL LENGTH	10' 3"	
OVERALL WIDTH	4' 2"	
OVERALL HEIGHT	3' 6·5"	

Scale ¼in to 1ft. Driving seat in central position. Cushions uncompressed.

PERFORMANCE

ACCELERATION:
Speed Range, Gear Ratios and Time in Sec.

M.P.H.	4.6 to 1	6.3 to 1	9.2 to 1	15.2 to 1
10—30	—	—	6.2	—
20—40	15.5	9.4	5.8	—
30—50	15.2	9.4	—	—
40—60	16.5	12.0	—	—

From rest through gears to:

M.P.H.			sec.
30	..	..	5.6
40	..	..	8.8
50	..	..	14.4
60	..	..	21.8
70	..	..	34.5

Standing quarter mile 22.4 sec.

MAXIMUM SPEEDS ON GEARS:

Gear			M.P.H.	K.P.H.
Top	..	(mean)	80	128.7
		(best)	83	133.6
3rd	..	..	70	112.6
2nd	..	..	49	78.9
1st	..	..	29	46.7

TRACTIVE EFFORT:

			Pull (lb per ton)	Equivalent Gradient
Top	..	..	105	1 in 21.2
Third	..	..	230	1 in 9.7
Second	..	..	300	1 in 7.4

BRAKES (at 30 m.p.h. in neutral):

Pedal load in lb	Retardation	Equivalent stopping distance in ft
25	0.20	152
50	0.47	64
75	0.65	46
85	0.93	32

FUEL CONSUMPTION:
M.P.G. at steady speeds

M.P.H.	Direct Top
30	63.5
40	57.2
50	46.5
60	37.7

Overall fuel consumption for 620 miles, 33.1 m.p.g. (8.6 litres per 100 km.).
Approximate normal range 31–43 m.p.g. (9.4–6.6 litres per 100 km.).
Fuel: Premium grade, with oil in the ratio of 16 to 1.

DIMENSIONS:
Wheelbase, 5ft 8.5in.
Track: F, 3ft 6.25in; R, 3ft 6in.
Length (overall): 10ft 3in.
Width, 4ft 2in (standard), 4ft 5in (over wheel trims).
Height, 3ft 6.5in (top of screen).
Ground clearance, 7in.

DATA

PRICE (basic), with two-seater body, **£432 9s.**
British purchase tax, **£217 11s.**
Total (in Great Britain), **£650.**
Extras: Luggage grid **£7 10s.**
Tonneau cover **£6 10s.**
Revolution counter **£8** (plus fitting).
Wheel rim trims **£4 10s.**

ENGINE: Capacity, 492 c.c. (30 cu in).
Number of cylinders, 3.
Bore and stroke, 58 × 62 mm (2.28 × 2.44 in).
Valve gear, ported two-stroke.
Compression ratio, 7.5 to 1.
B.H.P. 30 (gross) at 5,000 r.p.m. (B.H.P. per ton laden 56.8).
Torque, 35.4 lb ft at 3,500 r.p.m.
M.P.H. per 1,000 r.p.m. in top gear, 13.2.

WEIGHT (with 5 gals fuel): 7.5 cwt (847 lb).
Weight distribution (per cent): F, 64.5; R, 35.5.
Laden as tested, 10.5 cwt (1,183 lb).
Lb per c.c. (laden), 2.4.

BRAKES: Type, Girling.
Method of operation, hydraulic.
Drum dimensions: F, 7in diameter; 1.25in wide. R, 7in diameter; 1.25in wide.
Lining area: F, 32.5 sq in; R, 32.5 sq in (123.1 sq in per ton laden).

TYRES: 5.20—12 in Michelin Super-Comfort.
Pressures (lb sq in): F, 14; R, 12.

TANK CAPACITY: 5 Imperial gallons.
Cooling system, air-cooled, no fan.

STEERING : Turning circle:
Between kerbs, 27ft 2in.
Between walls, 28ft 8.5in.
Turns of steering wheel from lock to lock, 2¼.

ELECTRICAL SYSTEM: 12-volt; 22 ampère-hour battery.
Head lights, double dip; 24-24 watt bulbs.

SUSPENSION: Front, independent, wishbones with Girling coil spring and telescopic damper units.
Rear, independent, swing axles with Girling coil spring and telescopic damper units.

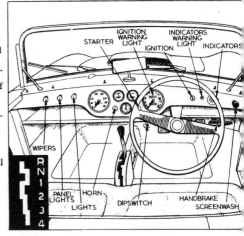

MINIATURE CARS
A Berkeley Four-seater

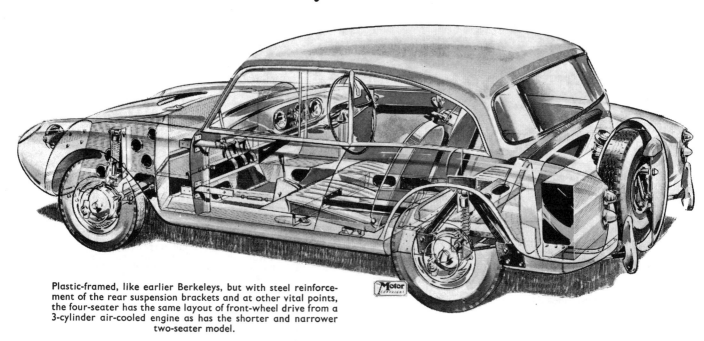

Plastic-framed, like earlier Berkeleys, but with steel reinforcement of the rear suspension brackets and at other vital points, the four-seater has the same layout of front-wheel drive from a 3-cylinder air-cooled engine as has the shorter and narrower two-seater model.

ADDED to the 1959 range of sporting miniatures built at Biggleswade by Berkeley Cars Ltd. is a four-seater model, which will be exhibited at Earls Court both in open form and with an optional lift-off plastic hard-top. At a price of under £700, including purchase tax, this roomier version of an ultra-light sporting car will have no direct competitors. As compared with the two-seater, the new model is claimed to be less than 1 cwt. heavier.

As our drawing shows, this is to be an extremely low and smart looking car, following on the lines of existing Berkeley models but longer and wider as well as incorporating improved details. It will be powered by the 492 c.c. Excelsior three-cylinder two-stroke engine now used in all Berkeleys, but to cater for greater loads which may be carried there is a heavy-duty gearbox and stronger driving chains. Four speeds and reverse are provided by the Albion gearbox, which has a central quadrant-type control, top gear ratio being 5.1/1 instead of the 4.65/1 hitherto used on two-seater cars.

For the new Berkeley, the ingenious use of a plastic body with glass fibre reinforcement as the chassis frame is continued, an increase of 8 in. in the wheelbase and of 3¾ in. in the track being accompanied by revisions of the shaping of the box-section side members to give extra strength. Moulded-in light alloy stiffeners are also supplemented by steel brackets to spread out concentrated loads from the rear suspension. At the front, wider spacing of

the coil-and-wishbone suspension assemblies has given the increased track, but the divided-axle I.R.S. is much improved by lowering of the pivot points for swinging half-axles, which are also of increased length. At front and rear, coil springs encircle either Armstrong or Girling telescopic shock absorbers.

Girling hydraulic brakes of 7-in. size are used on all wheels, the front brakes of two leading shoe pattern and the rear with supplementary cable operation from the pull-out handbrake. Steering is by a Burman gear of worm-and-nut design, a matching idler being used with a three-piece track rod, and bolt-on wheels of low weight carry 5.20-12 Michelin tyres. Silencing of the 3-cylinder two-stroke engine is a two-stage process, the individual exhaust stubs running tangentially into a baffled expansion chamber from which the exit is via a straight-through silencer lined with steel wool to an outlet beneath the car. Carburation of the air-cooled engine is by three Amal units, fed from a 5½-gallon rear petroil tank by S.U. electric pump. Access to the power unit is improved by making the front air intake grille lift up as a unit with the top of the alligator-pattern bonnet.

Extra width has permitted the installation of individual front seats in place of the bench seat of earlier Berkeley cars. There is now full trim inside the doors (which incorporate big pockets for maps etc.) and a removable instrument panel carries speedometer, fuel contents gauge, ammeter and (as an optional extra) a rev. counter.

Upholstery is in Vynide, and Hardura plastic carpets are used on the floor. Four different paint colours are available, and equipment includes a Siba 12-volt 90-watt Dynastart, dipping headlights, twin windscreen wipers, stop lamps, flashing turn indicators, and a tool kit.

As an alternative to the usual folding hood, a moulded plastic hard-top of pillarless design as shown in our drawing may be fitted to the four-seat Berkeley, this securing neatly to the curved-glass windscreen and incorporating a broad rear window. A somewhat similar removable hard-top is now available for two-seater Berkeleys also.

BERKELEY 4-SEATER

Cylinders			3, air-cooled
Bore			... 58 mm.
Stroke			... 62 mm.
Cubic capacity			492 c.c.
Piston area			... 12.3 sq. in.
Valves			None (2-stroke)
Compression ratio			7.5
Maximum power			... 30 b.h.p.
at			... 5,500 r.p.m.
Top gear ratio			5.1
Final drive			Chain to front wheels
Wheelbase			... 6 ft. 6 in.
Overall length			... 10 ft. 11 in.
Overall width			... 4 ft 6 in.
Height			... 3 ft. 10 in.
Turning circle			28 ft.
Dry weight			7 cwt.

45

1959 MODELS *Berkeley Foursome*

Enlarged Three-cylinder Sports Model: Detachable Hardtop Available

With hardtop and side-screens removed, it is transformed into an open car. The vertical spare wheel cover is secured by a single domed nut

IN THIS country no manufacturer has encouraged the cult of the small two-stroke-engined sports car more than Berkeley, who have met with sales success both at home and abroad with their two- and three-cylinder open two-seaters. Recently a hardtop version of this model has been added to the range. These diminutive front-wheel-drive machines have a surprising performance for their engine size, but to meet the needs of those owners who require rather more body space than the other models in the Berkeley range give, the new Foursome has now been introduced.

Extra room has been found by an increase of 8in in the wheelbase and 2in in the track, making it possible for a rear seat 35in wide to be placed between the rear wheel arches. It is not claimed by the manufacturers that this gives full four-seater accommodation, but the extra seat is comfortably upholstered and suitable for two children, or even for adults for a short journey. An advantage of the front-wheel drive layout is that the rear seat does not have to clear a normal axle, and on this new model space has been gained by lowering the attachment points of the pair of swinging wishbone-shaped rear suspension arms by 3½in. The combined coil spring-damper units for this rear suspension are carried outboard of the wheel arch diaphragms instead of inside, as on the smaller models.

A special feature of the Foursome is the detachable glass-fibre hardtop and the rigid-framed transparent plastic side windows which, when fitted, convert the open car into a saloon. A soft folding hood is supplied with the car, its supporting irons dropping into sockets in the panels beside the rear seat. The hood can be stowed in a bag, to rest on the rear decking. The side windows, of course, can also be used with this hood.

An interesting combination of glass-fibre reinforced polyester resin, aluminium and steel is used in the construction. It comprises three mouldings—a floor section, to which are secured the separate sections for front and rear of the body.

The lower moulding has box-section side channels reinforced by aluminium plates and angles riveted to it, and is further stiffened by steel and aluminium cross-members.

The front section of the body has an aluminium bulkhead behind the engine compartment, moulded into the glass-fibre. A steel superstructure integrated with this moulding, provides mountings for engine, transmission, front suspension, steering and pedals. At the rear, steel stiffeners are built into both the floor moulding and the rear section of the body at the wheel arch diaphragms, to provide pick-up points for mounting the rear suspension arms and coil spring-damper units.

Mounted transversely on rubber bushes ahead of the front wheel centres, the three-cylinder two-stroke Excelsior Talisman engine drives the front wheels through a multi-plate clutch, Albion four-speed and reverse gear box and roller chain final drive to a differential and jointed half shafts.

Front suspension is by unequal length wishbones, the combined coil spring-damper being above the upper wishbone.

Seats are placed very low in the body

[Labels on cutaway diagram:] SLIDING WINDOW · HARD TOP ATTACHMENT POINTS · REMOVABLE SPARE WHEEL COVER · 6 GALLON FUEL TANK · TURN INDICATORS · ATTACHMENT POINTS, UNDERBODY TO REAR MOULDING · SWING AXLE REAR SUSPENSION WITH COIL SPRING · STEEL SUSPENSION MOUNTING BRACKETS · GLASS FIBRE UNDERBODY WITH ALUMINIUM & STEEL REINFORCEMENT

SPECIFICATION

ENGINE: No. of cylinders, 3 in line (transverse); bore and stroke, 58 x 62 mm (2.28 x 2.44in); displacement, 492 c.c. (30.02 cu in); valve position, ported 2-stroke; compression ratio, 7.5 to 1; max. b.h.p. (gross), 30 at 5,500 r.p.m.; max. b.m.e.p., 89.5 lb sq in at 3,500 r.p.m.; max. torque, 35.6 lb ft at 3,500 r.p.m.; carburettors, 3 Amal; fuel pump, S.U. electric; tank capacity, 5¼ Imp. gallons (25 litres); cooling system, air cooled; battery, 12 volt, 32 amp hr.

TRANSMISSION: clutch, 5 7/16 in dia. Albion multi-plate; gear box, four speeds, central quadrant change; overall ratios, top 5.1, 3rd, 6.43, 2nd 9.15, 1st 15.1, reverse, 16.6; final drive, roller chain to front wheels, ratio 2.23 to 1.
CHASSIS: brakes, Girling hydraulic; drum dia. and shoe width, 7 x 1¼in; suspension, front coil spring and wishbones; rear, coil spring and single wishbone; dampers, Armstrong telescopic; wheels, disc, bolt-on; tyre size: 5.20–12in; steering, Burman worm and nut; steering wheel, 2-spoke 16in dia., turns lock to lock, 2¼.

DIMENSIONS: wheelbase, 6ft 6in (198.1 cm); track: front, 3ft 10¼in (117.5 cm), rear, 3ft 10in (116.8 cm); overall length, 10ft 11in (332.7 cm); overall width, 4ft 6in (137.2 cm); overall height, 3ft 10in (116.8 cm); ground clearance, 7in (17.8 cm); turning circle, 28ft (8.53 m); kerb weight, 7 cwt (356 kg) approx.

PERFORMANCE DATA: top gear m.p.h. at 1,000 r.p.m., 13.2; torque lb ft per cu in engine capacity, 1.19; brake surface area swept by linings, 110 sq in.

and the front pair have a very simple adjustment. For each seat this consists of a pair of brackets fixed to the floor, each having four slots, into any of which a bar beneath the rear of the seat can be dropped. The front seat cushions have tension-springs and foam rubber over-lays. Upholstery is in Vynide through-out and the floor is covered with durable plastic carpets.

Beneath the scuttle is a full-width tray for small luggage, and there is a further small space behind the rear seat squab, in front of and to the right of the fuel tank. The doors are 2in wider than on the smaller Berkeley, and have concealed

Above left : The front passenger's seat tips forward for access to the rear, where a well-upholstered seat has sufficient head- and leg-room for two children, or an adult for a short journey. Above right: An idea can be obtained of the low overall height of the new Berkeley with hardtop by com-paring it with the nose of an Austin A.40

Instruments are grouped in a central panel; a rev counter is an optional extra, desirable with a free-revving engine. There is a simplified gear change quadrant

hinges. Openings in the trim panels pro-vide pockets for oddments. Interior door handles only are fitted, reached from out-side by opening the sliding panels in the side window. The frame of the curved screen is fixed to the body, and the glass-fibre hardtop is secured to it by eleven

screws. At the rear, the attachment is by two wing nuts and four screws.

A top speed of 75 m.p.h. is claimed for the Foursome, which costs £465 10s basic, £699 12s with purchase tax, increased to £484 8s and £727 19s respectively if the hardtop is ordered.

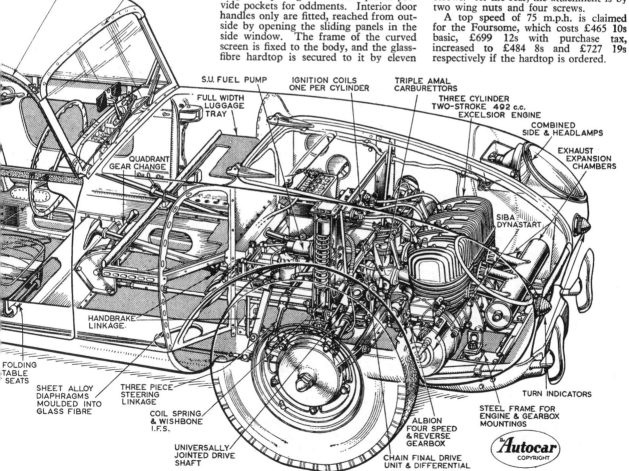

REMOVABLE GLASS FIBRE HARD TOP & SIDE SCREENS

HARD TOP ATTACHMENT POINTS

S.U. FUEL PUMP

FULL WIDTH LUGGAGE TRAY

IGNITION COILS ONE PER CYLINDER

TRIPLE AMAL CARBURETTORS

THREE CYLINDER TWO-STROKE 492 c.c. EXCELSIOR ENGINE

COMBINED SIDE & HEADLAMPS

EXHAUST EXPANSION CHAMBERS

QUADRANT GEAR CHANGE

SIBA DYNASTART

HANDBRAKE LINKAGE.

FOLDING TABLE SEATS

SHEET ALLOY DIAPHRAGMS MOULDED INTO GLASS FIBRE

THREE PIECE STEERING LINKAGE

COIL SPRING & WISHBONE I.F.S.

UNIVERSALLY JOINTED DRIVE SHAFT

ALBION FOUR SPEED & REVERSE GEARBOX

CHAIN FINAL DRIVE UNIT & DIFFERENTIAL

TURN INDICATORS

STEEL FRAME FOR ENGINE & GEARBOX MOUNTINGS

The Autocar
COPYRIGHT

V. R. BERRIS

BERKELEY'S BUSY BABY

By DOUG BLAIN

The 328 c.c. Berkeley, smallest production sports car in the world, is a challenge. In this evaluation, tester Doug Blain makes no bones about revealing the little car's bad points as well as its good ones.

Excelsior Talisman Twin two-stroke engine drives front wheels, is beautifully accessible. Carburetion is by twin Amals, fuel is gravity fed. Our car could have done with more bonnet sealing.

SOME people will look at the Berkeley and yell with laughter. Others might feel inclined to perform a gracious salaam before its trim, mesh alloy grille.

Us? We're keeping out of this!

Frankly we were apprehensive as, test trappings bundled in a thick sweater under our right arm, we approached the John Crouch (Aust.) Ltd. service station in Sydney for this month's S.C.W. road test. No one we knew had owned one of these tiny, 18 b.h.p. English sports cars, nor even driven one. Down-to-earth test data on the 328 c.c., Excelsior-engined model was hard to come by. We were ready for anything.

From kerbside and Motor Show observances we knew the Berkeley to be very, very small. We knew it to be pretty. We knew it to be expensive.

Our car (we almost tripped over it as we approached the showroom) was sky blue with grey upholstery and hood. It had worked all day as a demonstrator when we took over, and at first we mistook metropolitan grime for bad finish on the fibreglass body. A quick rub with a duster back at the office reassured us—the finish was excellent.

Clambering inside, we listened carefully while Crouch sales manager Bill Reynolds explained the distinctly unorthodox controls. Getting in, by the way, was a rum old effort. We're over two yards long, the Berkeley stands just 3 ft. 7½ in. top to toe, and the hood was up.

Carefully hidden—don't ask us why — under the dash was the

choke lever, a delightfully positive control that should be thrust under the nose of every manufacturer on both sides of the Equator. On the left of the panel was the two-position switch for side and headlights, with the horn button beside it. Then came the ignition key and the Dynastart button. To the right again was the panel light switch, which illuminates the speedometer only.

On the whole the dash is a neat one, but (a) horn and starter buttons are exactly similar and very close (consequences can be amusing as well as annoying) and (b) the auxiliary instrument panel, containing fuel gauge and ammeter, is unnecessarily flimsy. A word about keys here too. Berkeley are not alone in supplying three, one for ignition, another for bonnet, and a third for boot. They're the same shape and entirely unnecessary in our view. The confusion at night is hopeless.

The cockpit itself is excellently designed, providing amazingly good accommodation for two adults. The boot is a lidded well behind the seats, with a trapdoor that leads through into the extreme tail of the car. The factory brochure says it's possible to carry children in the foremost of the two compartments, we assume with the lid up. We took their word for it.

The seat is an ingenious affair of padded, quilted plastic over rubber thongs. It is neat, comfortable, and takes up very little room. The effect when you're sitting two abreast is of twin individual seats, although the quilted overlay reaches right across the car and

two smallish children can replace an adult passenger. The Berkeley is as restful on a long journey as any open car we've struck.

Legroom is limited, but enough. For once in a small car the pedals are right where they should be and not canted over to the left. Their size is just right, and heel and toe gearchanging is simple although unnecessary. The pedals should have rubber covers.

Most of our cynical apprehension about the Berkeley disappeared after a very few city miles. The clutch is terrifying at first, but when you get used to it the whole transmission mechanism becomes a delight to use. The motorcycle-type gearbox has no synchromesh, and is the better for the omission. To change ratios you simply slam the stubby central lever towards or away from you (depending on whether you're changing up or down) until it hits something. Selection speed is limited only by your deftness with the left foot. On the whole the mechanism works like an automatic transmission selector, only it's much sturdier and there are positive stops between gears.

Reverse is engaged in a roundabout sort of way, but at least it is there.

Note that we haven't lamented the lack of a tachometer. The reason is that it's entirely unwarranted. Accelerating through the gears with the Berkeley is

simply a matter of treading on the right pedal and changing up when the lusty little two-cylinder, two-stroke motor will rev no more. Our car had a bad habit of four-stroking (technical name for that b-r-r-r noise your lawnmower makes when it's flat out) when all the stops were out. The cure, which worked well within limits, was to ease off slightly—whereupon the motor began to pile on revs again.

In all fairness though, we must say that our car needed attention in the motor department, and we were adequately briefed about it beforehand. It seems that Berkeleys as they come from the ships are tuned for English atmospheric conditions, which require a richer mixture than ours. They are not altered until the mileage reaches about 500, since the distributors maintain that the richness helps running in. Consequently performance on a properly tuned and thoroughly "freed-up" car could be quite a bit better.

Not that the Berkeley is embarrassingly slow. On the contrary, its performance is amazingly good —with a few minor reservations.

It pans out this way. Straight acceleration is undeniably slow on the stopwatch, but because of the little car's healthy exhaust crackle, its nearness to the ground and its generally sporty feel — not to mention its airiness with the hood down — it seems to be going a lot

BERKELEY'S BUSY BABY

faster on the drag strip than almost any other car we can think of at anywhere near the price. And isn't that the important thing, after all? We're asking you.

The Berkeley sets its own pace. You keep your foot pretty close to the floor and it hums along as happy as a lark, usually at around 50 m.p.h.

Once in its stride it will pass anything that gets in the way, much to the consternation of the car-proud and the wealthy. It is a car for the enthusiast, the driver who's young at heart and delights in fresh air and plenty of it, in getting the best from an extremely small piece of internal combustion engineering, in cornering absolutely on the limit all the time in complete safety and almost complete freedom from crippling tyre and fuel bills.

Cornering is nothing short of amazing, largely because of the car's combination of front wheel drive, independent all-round suspension (swing axles at the rear), and Michelin X tyres.

Technique is to approach a bend as fast as the car will go, ease off slightly just as you enter, keep well out at the approach and then give her all she's got through the apex and out the other side. Speed through a given corner in the Berkeley has nothing to do with roll centres, centre of gravity or kneel — it depends entirely on adhesion. Understandably, since it's quite possible for one man to lift the back end right off the ground, the tail will break away quite easily on a slippery or wet surface. For instance at one stage during our test we chased an Austin-Healey two up through a series of fast bends. We held him quite comfortably until Monsieur the Healey Driver decided to take to the inside verge, scattering gravel over the marble-smooth roadway. The bend was a fast one, and the round pebbles got us into trouble with rear wheel adhesion. Nothing serious, mind — the Berkeley stayed with us through 300 miles of rapid motoring and remained controllable every inch of the way — but enough to lose us that rather unequal battle.

The differential, mounted in the extreme nose of the car, works on the ZF limited slip principle. Wheelspin is almost non-existant, even in loose gravel at full bore in first.

There is pronounced transmission snatch on full lock under power, but it is not harmful and after awhile you begin to allow for it when making U-turns. Turning circle is excellent, but not amazing.

If the Berkeley's cornering is excellent, the brakes are nothing

Berkeley (pronounce it Bar-cley) dash is neat, reasonably comprehensive considering two-stroke motor. Auxiliary panel containing fuel gauge and ammeter is a trifle flimsy, we thought. Note panic handles on windscreen.

British-made Berkeley glass fibre sports car has cleanliness of appearance that many bigger manufacturers could copy. Lights are hidden behind streamlined plastic covers, bonnet opens forward.

Berkeley's lines are so well balanced that only a direct contrast can show its tiny size. Tyres are Michelins, help roadholding tremendously. Wheel size: 12 in.

BERKELEY: Specifications:

POWER UNIT

Type .... two cyl., side by side
Valve arrangement ..... Automatic, two-stroke
Bore and stroke .... 58 x 62 mm.
Displacement .... 328 c.c.
Compression ratio .... 8.2 to 1
Compression ratio .... twin Amals
Max. b.h.p. at r.p.m. ..... 18.2 at 5,250
(approx.)

CHASSIS:

Wheelbase .... 5 ft. 10 in.
Max. track .... 3 ft. 8 in.
Suspension, front
wishbones with Girling spring/damper
units

Suspension, rear
independent, swing axles with Girling
units

Steering .... worm and peg
Steering, turns lock to lock .... $2\frac{1}{4}$
Turning circle .... 26 ft. 6 in. (right),
29 ft. (left)
Tyre size .... 5.20 x 12 in.

GENERAL:

Fuel capacity .... $3\frac{1}{2}$ Imp. gallons
Weight, dry
$6\frac{1}{2}$ cwt. Laden as tested, $7\frac{3}{4}$ cwt.
Brakes .... Girling hydraulic
Brakes, lining area .... 65 sq. in.

Performance:

TOP SPEED:

Two-way average .... 65 m.p.h.
Fastest one way .... 69 m.p.h.

ACCELERATION:

Zero to   seconds
30 m.p.h. 7.9
40 m.p.h. 16.7
50 m.p.h. 25.1
Standing $\frac{1}{4}$-mile 26.8

SPEEDS IN GEARS:

I .... 0-22 m.p.h.
II .... 10-38 m.p.h.
III .... 15-70 m.p.h.

FUEL CONSUMPTION:

Hard driven .... 46.3 m.p.g.
Normal driving .... 57.4 m.p.g.

BERKELEY'S BUSY BABY

short of superb. Working on 12-inch wheels, they will stop the car in an almost embarrassingly short space from any speed. The feeling at the pedal under normal conditions is one of smooth, progressive stopping rather than that fierce sensation that smacks of soft linings and super sales technique. Jump on the pedal and the car will pull up so violently that sheer decelerative force tends to hurl the tail around towards the obstruction. For that reason hard braking on a corner is no more to be recommended than it is with an ordniary car, although limited indulgence is quite permissible.

Low speed torque is not outstanding. At the wheel of the Berkeley you work fairly consistently at the gear box. Steep hills force a change down, but it's fun to use the cogs, not a hardship. Because of the tiny engine size there is very little retardation on the over-run and the brakes have to be used quite hard.

Steering is one thing you don't have to work at. In fact, it's so light that you can almost forget the wheel and resort to steering with the throttle. A bare touch will change the car's direction at any speed from a crawl to the downhill maximum of roughly 75 m.p.h.

Rain brings trouble with a car as small as this. The roadholding remains impeccable, but every car that passes you or refuses to surrender the crown of the road hurls an absolute bath of filthy water over screen and side curtains. The wipers don't help much — their blades are too short and they move too slowly. The only solution in really heavy traffic is to lean out every now and then and wipe the screen with a cloth.

Luggage space in the Berkeley is good, considering. A vast shelf under the dash will take anything from a soft overnight bag to the spare wheel, the boot holds several more bags (less if the hood is in there too), and both doors boast substantial pockets. The fuel tank, which holds enough petrol mixture for just over 200 miles of touring motoring at 60 m.p.g., is under the bonnet. It should be bigger.

Well, that's the Berkeley. If you're young and adventurous, or think you are, and if you seek really low-cost motoring with a distinctly sporting flavour, lots of fresh air, lots of noise, and very few home comforts, then you can't do better at any price.

If you're not as young as you used to be and you've a hankering after rapid, silent transport in armchair surroundings, then put your £845 towards something else. And what the heck do you think you're doing reading this anyway?

For our part, we look forward eagerly to testing the 500 c.c. Berkeley in the very near future.

Ratchet gearchange is simple, efficient. Reverse is at top, then comes neutral, first. Picture shows lever at second gear stop. For top you pull it down to the floor.

Berkeley de Luxe

MORE ROOM AT THE BACK : BETTER FORWARD
VISION : STIFFER SPRINGING FORE AND AFT

THERE is a new Berkeley three-wheeler—a de-luxe version of the basic T60 model. Called T60/4, the newcomer has better rear-seat accommodation, which means more legroom for children, or more luggage space. There is a larger hood and improved forward vision. Both front and rear suspensions are strengthened and a larger spring-and-hydraulic unit is used at the rear; advantage is taken of this to lower the seating position without risk of bottoming. Discs are fitted to the front wheels.

In all other respects the de-luxe model is identical with the standard version. The glass-reinforced plastic body is bonded to a framework of light-alloy bulkheads and cross members. Rear-wheel springing is by an arm pivoted on two bonded-rubber bushes and controlled by a single Armstrong telescopic strut. At the front there are wishbones of unequal length, controlled by Armstrong struts. Each wheel carries a 5.20 × 12in tyre and incorporates a 7in-diameter Girling brake operated hydraulically; the front brakes have double leading shoes.

Under the bonnet is a 328 c.c. (58 × 62mm) Excelsior air-cooled twin two-stroke engine driving through an Albion gear box with four speeds and reverse. A chain takes the drive to a differential connected to the front wheels by universally jointed shafts.

Body colour may be chosen from red, yellow, dark green, light blue and Old English White. Black or brown may be specified for the Vynide upholstery.

Basic price of the T60/4 is £351 5s 2d; with British purchase tax the total is £425. Price of the T60 remains at £399 19s 11d (including £69 8s 7d p.t.). A hardtop variant of the standard model costs £412 10s (including £71 11s 9d p.t.) and it is planned to market the de-luxe model in hardtop form soon.

Makers are Berkeley Cars, Ltd., Hitchin Street, Biggleswade, Berks.

The top picture shows the de-luxe Berkeley three-wheeler with its improved windscreen and wheel discs. Below is shown the rear seat which provides more leg room for children, or greater luggage space, than on earlier Berkeley models

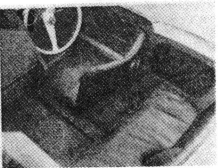

THIS TEST hammered one thing home to us—don't even try to drive fast, let alone race, unless your car is in top shape. And the only way you can guarantee this is by assuming that nothing has been done. And if the car is a new one, this goes double.

We picked up our 500cc Berkeley from Tony Pompeo's, located on W. 19th Street so close to the water that the unloading booms practically lower the cars right into his shop. The car is the property of John deGarmo, who lent it to us for the test, and it was too new. It wasn't until the second day we had it that we washed the dust from it. We didn't give Tony enough time to prepare it, deciding to take our chances. After all, how much can a new car need?

Well, first it needs a thousand miles of running in, and this we gave it. In the course of the thousand miles we discovered (1) the battery was discharged on the boat and needed recharging (2) the shifting linkage was not adjusted properly. To downshift into third, you had to go into second and then come back, and (3) the clutch will slip under power unless it is adjusted.

A few months ago John deGarmo notified us that Berkeley Cars, Ltd. were about to get both feet into racing by way of factory options. Simply stated, this meant a hop-up kit.

Here are the steps the factory suggests. All mating surfaces in the induction system are to be fitted. This includes aligning the transfer ports of the cylinder and the crankcase, trimming of the base of the cylinder to match the larger entrance to the transfer port, and enlargement and polishing of the transfer port itself to allow earlier entry of a larger volume of gas. The enlargement is done by means of factory-provided templates. The polishing is very awkward to do, a curved file being required, but as the tuning pamphlet says, "patience and care are well repaid in an improved performance."

Berkeley Cars, Ltd. now have both feet in class racing. Properly set up with factory options, the 500cc'er can be a class winner. For the casual strictly-as-a-hobby entrant, it provides the most fun return for dollar investment.

BERKELEY 500

DUAL-PURPOSE SPORTS CARS FOR 1959

Remember that the Berkeley is powdered by a two-stroke engine. As such it has no valves and no cam. Ports, or shaped holes, in the walls of the cylinders scavenge exahust gases and admit a fresh charge. The timing at which this takes place is a function of the vertical placement of the intake and exhaust ports both in relation to TDC and to each other, and of the length and shape of the piston skirt. Thus, altering the piston skirt or enlarging these holes on the vertical plane is the direct equivalent to putting a hot cam into a four-stroke engine.

Now that the cylinder has been modified, it is necessary to correspondingly modify the piston. An optional Super Sports piston has narrower rings (to postpone flutter) and provision for better lubrication at higher revs. The skirts of the pistons are then filed away to correspond to the newly-shaped ports. As a final machine job, the head is planed a sixteenth to bring the compression ratio up to the capabilities of modern American fuel.

Exhaust tuning is a ticklish proposition with a two-stroke engine. We watched a Berkeley driver once as he made a straight-through exhaust system, which he assumed would give him more power because it removed all back pressure. He couldn't get enough power from the engine to put the car in motion. Never use a four-stroke's tuned exhaust system, as two-stroke engine requirements are entirely different. A two-stroke seems to thrive on a little back pressure. The factory recommends the expansion chamber that extends across the front of the engine on the late '58 models.

Everything is clearly spelled out, so we

had only one difficulty. It seems that nothing but advice had reached this side of the water. We had no templates. We had to confine ourselves to what we could get from 500 very-strictly-stock cc's.

When we road tested the 328 cc Berkeley last February, we stated that another 172 cc would be a welcome addition. It was a surprising addition. Pulling onto the Connecticut Thruway, we took the 500 cc'er up to 50 mph in second, and seventy in third. We were truly surprised by the response, and the "big" Berkeley has no trouble keeping up with the traffic. Cutting off onto route 7, and motoring over the twists and turns to Lime Rock, the smallness of the car was a big asset: the road was proportionately twice as wide. And the lightweight machine, with its gutty engine powering into the front wheels, is a remarkably good road machine. But it is different.

On the track, we adhered to the rules that govern the operation of front-wheel-driven vehicles at speed, with one exception. We kept the foot throttle on the floor, but we did not reach over to tap the brake with the left foot. It was absolutely unnecessary. With one exception—the end of the long straight—no braking was needed.

Tossing the Berkeley into turns, one is aware that the rear end is exceedingly light. Perhaps you will remember the road test of the 328 cc version, when one of our editors picked up the rear end; he did it with the 500 cc model, too. This lightness is not an evil *per se*, however it does require careful handling. You get the feeling that once the rear starts out—and it goes out suddenly—it's going to go out all the way. But the same lightness that allows it to go out makes it very easy to bring back. We never had any real trouble, but we were prepared for it if it did come along.

The car is a tracker. The rear wants to follow the front around, and it will do so as long as enough power is going into the front wheels to pull. But a sudden side bite, induced by cutting the wheel sharply into the corner, causes the rear wheels to go out just as suddenly. Getting off the accelerator is a mistake: you have to ease off on the steering lock. Like many front wheel drive cars, its understeering and oversteering characteristics vary with throttle opening.

Lap times: we really don't want to give any. The engine was not loose enough for us to stand on it for extended duration, and its stiffness kept it from winding to its potential. In addition, competition conditions induced a little slippage in the clutch. If we had the time we would have adjusted it; but we didn't. We toured the circuit rapidly, and nearly managed to keep up with bigger machinery that was touring in the same manner. It was apparent, however, that an engine utilizing the factory options will go a lot quicker, both on the straights and through the turns. Properly handled by a driver experienced in the car, the 500 cc Berkeley can be a serious race car.

But just as important is the psychology of racing the Berkeley. It's an ideal machine for the hobbyist racer. Whether you win or lose—and with preparation you can win—you'll have a ball. You'll get a tremendous fun return for your investment.

—*lfg*

As with most front-wheel driven cars, steer characteristics are a function of throttle opening. The Berkeley tracks; however rear can be induced to break away suddenly.

So light that three men can literally pick up and carry the car, the 500cc three-barrel two-stroker has plenty of guts and go. With the hop-up kit, it's a lively competitor that can win.

Tuned exhausts from four-strokes don't do it; two-strokes thrive on a little back pressure. There's always room for experimentation.

By DOUG BLAIN

BERKELEY *grows up*

. . . the baby has become a real challenge

WHEELS gives Sydney's first 500-c.c. Berkeley the once-over, finds it a midge with more than a little sting. Should give the opposition a big fright, we're thinking . . .

LAST time we drove a Berkeley (SPORTS CAR WORLD, December) we looked forward publically with more than a little enthusiasm to the day we could sample the new 500 c.c. model. That day has arrived.

Superficially, the two cars look identical. It's only when you peer closely that you notice the wider door openings and tail-end petrol filler (outside), changed dashboard and upholstery (inside) and three-cylinder engine (under the bonnet).

But the changes are all significant, and that new motor really does give the Berkeley amazing smoothness and acceleration as well as extremely good top-gear flexibility. At £975, including tax, the revised model costs only £130 more than the older car, which continues in production.

Let's begin by driving the 500.

Clutch action is still abrupt, in the real vintage manner. But you soon get used to that. The gearbox has grown into a four-speed job,

but the makers have retained the classic constant-mesh, no synchromesh pattern we commented on so favourably earlier. The change is positive and among the quickest in current production anywhere in the world. Literally, you flick your wrist to change gears in the Berkeley, smacking the lever back in its ratchet until you hear the healthy click as it meets the gate which separates the gears.

Ratios are really well spaced, and because of the Berkeley's extremely

Berkeley's lines are so trim that it's almost impossible to judge its tiny size from a picture. Number plate (we're sorry it's crooked) affords some comparison. Neat wheel discs look even better than wire.

New, wide doors give easy access. Seats are very comfortable, tray under dash holds lots of odds and ends or even the spare wheel!

Interior of latest version is classy, simple and neat. Blank space at left aches for tacho, however. Note four-speed gearchange.

wheels
NEW CAR TRYOUT

light weight they can be close without fear of take-off judder in bottom. You can play tunes on this box at 30 m.p.h. without even bothering to double de-clutch.

Top gear flexibility is quite amazing. We put the Berkeley at a really fierce city hill during our short, pre-release drive and it climbed cheerfully in top where many others would fear to tread in anything higher than second — from little more than 15 m.p.h., too.

Secret of this new-found urge is the Berkeley's 492 c.c. in-line, three-cylinder Excelsior motor. It's a two-stroke unit with bore and stroke 58 x 62 m.m., making it considerably over square. Triple Amal Monobloc carburettors help it to turn out some 30 b.h.p. at 5,500 r.p.m., and account to some extent for the tiny car's flexibility. This is, incidentally, getting on for twice the output of the 328 c.c. Excelsior Talisman fitted to the cheaper model. Maximum speed is a claimed 80 m.p.h.

A weight of only 6½ cwt. gives the Berkeley the distinction of having a power output in the order of 92 b.h.p. per ton.

Roadholding, thanks to all-independent suspension (coil/damper swing axles at the back) and Michelin-X 5.20 x 12 in. tyres, should be equal to the performance. Our jaunt showed that the springing is just as contemptuous of right-angle bends at 40 m.p.h. as it was in the old model. In fact this Berke-

ley must be just about the nippiest city car it's possible to own. Front wheel drive, of course.

The brakes are phenomenal. Applied hard, they will pull the car up with such violence that the tail leaves the ground and tends to swing round to meet the front if the front wheels are pointing anywhere but straight ahead.

Inside, the Berkeley is a much improved little car. Gone are the narrow, hip-squeezer doors and flimsy dash panel. You slide in through doors that are quite happy to admit a six-footer's thigh bone after he's seated himself. Seats are re-vamped, too. They still feature

the excellent rubber thong Pullman construction, but on the latest model they're neatly covered in a thick, smooth material that looks like leather but isn't. Very comfortable, what's more.

The new dash panel has a big 120 m.p.h. (what are you laughing at?) speedometer right in front of the driver and an ammeter and fuel gauge spaced out beside it. The space opposite the speedo is filled with a gauze grille, and looks as if it's just aching for a tachometer. Knobs are nicely spaced, and the horn button and starter are no longer side by side.

Continued on page 59

This is what gives the little Berkeley its urge. Excelsior three-cylinder, air-cooled two-cycle motor is as smooth as most sixes. Hefty expansion box up front keeps it reasonably quiet, too.

BERKELEY

Royal Enfield Four-stroke

Engine for a

British

Miniature

Sports

Car

AFTER concentrating for 2½ years on miniature sports cars with two-stroke engines, Berkeley Cars, Ltd., are now introducing a four-stroke engine for their existing range of models. Installation of a Royal Enfield 692 c.c. twin-cylinder engine gives these already lively little cars a 33% increase in power, brief experience at the wheel of a prototype disclosing quite exceptionally rapid acceleration from standstill. Price of the B95 2-seater is £659 inclusive, while the Q95 2-4-seater and QB95 long-wheelbase 2-seater both cost £714.

Familiar to motorcyclists, the Royal Enfield " Super Meteor " engine is a parallel twin-cylinder air-cooled unit: thermocouple testing is stated to have confirmed that the Berkeley installation with a generous front air intake and an air outlet on top of the bonnet provides ample cooling without need of a fan. Inclined overhead valves are operated by pushrods and rockers, there is a single horizontal Amal carburetter and ignition is by Lucas coil and distributor. Inside the engine the crankshaft is supported on one ball-type and one roller-type main bearing, but split plain-bearing connecting rods are used. The cast crankshaft incorporates integral balance weights and a central flywheel between the two cylinders, the Berkeley installation also incorporating an enclosed toothed flywheel on the output end of the crankshaft to permit use of a conventional electrical starter: a belt-driven 12-volt dynamo replaces the alternator used on motorcycles.

A light-alloy casting encloses the primary chain, which has an adjustable pad on its non-drive lower run to regulate tension. As hitherto, a Burman motorcycle-pattern clutch and gearbox assembly running at less than engine speed is used, but with four forward speeds and a reverse gear controlled by a central lever moving along a notched fore-and-aft quadrant, stronger gears catering for the new engine's increased torque. A duplex chain which links the gearbox to the frame-mounted differential is lubricated by oil mist from an engine breather.

As before, the Berkeley is of combined body-chassis construction, the main strength coming from the resin-bonded glass-fibre panels. A certain amount of reinforcement by sheet aluminium bulkheads is provided, and a steel cross-member carries the wishbone-type I.F.S. Steel extension brackets now run forward from each side of this front cross-member, and on them are two widely spaced Metalastik rubber engine mountings which support a crosstube bolted to the front of the engine. The third flexible mounting for the power unit is a rubber cone located below the differential, and although the new engine is of a type which is less well balanced mechanically than is the

BERKELEY B95

ENGINE

Cylinders	..	2 vertical, with two bearing crankshaft transversely mounted.
Bore and Stroke		70 mm. x 90 mm. (2.76 in. x 3.54 in.)
Cubic capacity	..	692 c.c. (42.3 cu. in.)
Piston area		11.9 sq. in.
Compression ratio		7½/1.
Valvegear	..	Inclined o.h.v. operated by pushrods and rockers.
Fuel system	..	Amal carburetter, fed by S.U. electrical fuel pump from 3½-gallon rear-mounted tank.
Ignition	..	Lucas coil.
Lubrication	..	Royal Enfield dry-sump system, with oil tank integral with crankcase and twin plunger-type oil pumps.
Cooling	.. ..	Air.
Electrical system		12 volt, with Lucas starter and belt-driven dynamo charging 32 amp. hr. accumulator.
Maximum power		40 b.h.p. at 5,500 r.p.m. equivalent to 137 lb./sq. in. b.m.e.p. at 3,250 ft./min. piston speed and 3.36 b.h.p. per sq. in. of piston area.
Maximum torque		42.5 lb. ft. at 4,000 r.p.m., equivalent to 177 lb./sq. in. b.m.e.p. at 2,360 ft./min. piston speed.

TRANSMISSION

Clutch	..	Albion multiplate in unit with gearbox.
Gearbox	..	Albion 4-speed and reverse with direct top gear and quadrant change, driven by enclosed chain from engine.
Overall ratios		4.31, 5.95, 8.62 and 13.7 ; reverse, 14.05.
Final drive	..	Open duplex chain from gearbox to frame-mounted differential, and universally jointed drive shafts to front wheels.

CHASSIS

Brakes	..	Girling 7-inch hydraulic, 2 leading shoes in front drums.
Brake areas	..	65 sq. in. of lining area working on 110 sq. in. rubbed area of drums.
Front suspension		Independent by transverse wishbones and coil springs mounted on telescopic dampers.
Rear suspension.		Independent by swinging half-axles and coil springs mounted on telescopic dampers.
Wheels and tyres		5.20-12 Michelin tyres on 5-stud bolt-on wheels.
Steering	..	Burman worm and nut.

DIMENSIONS

Length	..	Overall 10 ft. 3 in.; wheelbase 5 ft. 10 in.
Width	..	Overall 4 ft. 2 in.; Track 3 ft. 6¼ in.
Height	..	Overall 3 ft. 10 in.; ground clearance 6 in.
Turning circle	..	28 ft. diameter
Kerb weight	..	Approx. 7¼ cwt. (unladen but with oil, spare wheel, etc.)

EFFECTIVE GEARING

Top gear ratio	..	14.3 m.p.h. at 1,000 r.p.m. and 24.2 m.p.h. at 1,000 ft./min. piston speed.
Maximum torque.		4,000 r.p.m. corresponds to 57 m.p.h. in top gear.
Maximum power.		5,500 r.p.m. corresponds to 79 m.p.h. in top gear.
Probable top gear pulling power	..	295 lb./ton approx. (Computed by The Motor from Manufacturer's figures for torque gear ratio and kerb weight, with allowances for 3½ cwt. load, 10% losses and 60 lb./ton drag.)

BERKELEY QB95 AND Q95

Specification as above, except for :—Overall length 10 ft. 11 in.; wheelbase 6 ft. 6 in. ; Overall width 4 ft. 6 in. ; track 3 ft. 10¼ in.

BERKELEY

ACCESSIBLE through a new front-hinged type of bonnet, the Royal Enfield twin-cylinder engine is transversely mounted and drives the front wheels.

two-stroke unit, the flexibility in a combination of two high-placed front mountings and one low-placed rear mounting has given reasonable smoothness of running, down to 20 m.p.h. in top gear or up to a speedometer 70 m.p.h. in 3rd gear.

No change is being made in the 7-inch brakes, which are of the type used on touring cars weighing twice as much as the Berkeley. The new model is entirely distinctive in appearance, a higher bonnet line and rectangular cooling air intake grille going with the new and rather taller engine which is placed well

ahead of the front wheels, and fresh headlamp arrangements dispensing with the sloped plastic headlamp covers hitherto used.

Only 2-seat versions of the new Berkeley are being shown at Geneva, it being available with or without a " hard-top " for the open body. The new engine will shortly also be available in the slightly longer and wider type of car which was added to the range last autumn, this model being available either as the Q95 occasional 4-seater or as an extra roomy two-seater with very generous luggage capacity (type QB95).

BERKELEY GROWS UP

Continued from page 57

The windscreen supports form useful panic handles. The handbrake is under the dash, with the winker control handily placed above it, and the steering wheel on the car we tried was black, not white as before. It matched the upholstery. Exterior paint, just for the record, was just about the brightest red we've ever seen.

The wiper blades still want lengthening, please.

The Berkeley has, as most people know, a fibreglass body. Altogether it is very satisfactory. Finish has improved out of sight in comparison with the earliest examples, and now it's hard to tell the difference from steel. Until you can pick up the back end without so much as a grunt. Aluminium strengthening panels are mostly hidden under the skin, but they're pretty much in

evidence around the engine bay. Very nicely engineered, too.

Because the petrol tank is now at the back, luggage accommodation on this newest of Berkeleys has suffered somewhat.

You can still carry a kid in the boot, though, in lieu of a bag and the shelf under the dash is big enough to take the spare wheel and a good deal more besides. Both doors have pockets.

Nevertheless, a luggage rack as standard equipment would be nice.

Summing up: Ridiculous as it may seem, this infinitessimal sports car really does provide thoroughly safe, fast and comfortable transport for two. It is real fun to drive, has tons of urge, and petrol consumption (not to mention first cost) is just about as low as you'll get. Distributors: John Crouch (Aust.) Ltd., Sydney. ●

A New Sports Three-wheeler

THE BERKELEY MAKES ITS BOW

LATEST recruit to the growing ranks of three-wheeler manufacturers is the Berkeley concern, of Biggleswade, Beds—famous for 14 years as makers of high-quality caravans and latterly as builders of small front-wheel-driven sports car. This factory is now in production with a three-wheeled version of the car, powered by a 328 c.c. twin two-stroke Excelsior engine. With ultra-modern styling, chassis-less glass-fibre construction and a top speed of 55 to 60 m.p.h., the new Berkeley is listed at £330 11s. 3d. plus £69 8s. 8d. P.T., totalling a penny under £400.

Most road-users are familiar with the nippy little Berkeley four-wheelers, approximately 3,000 of which are already in service, some with the 328 c.c. twin engine, some with the same manufacturer's larger three-cylinder two-stroke unit, and others with a 700 c.c. o.h.v. vertical-twin Royal Enfield power plant of either "Meteor" or "Super Constellation" type. From the nose rearward as far as the seat-back, the three-wheeler is practically identical with the car, most of the parts being interchangeable. Both production and servicing of the newcomer have therefore been simplified considerably—with a consequent reduction of costs.

The three-wheeler's bodywork consists of three glass-fibre main sections bolted together. The first may be described as a long, narrow "dish." or "punt," forming the base of the entire structure and built up at the rear to house the single back wheel. Longitudinal and transverse box sections in light alloy are riveted to the glass fibre as strengtheners.

The front body moulding comprises, in one piece, the wings, bonnet, scuttle, dash, headlamp housings and hinge posts for the two 30-in.-wide doors. Bonded into it are further light-alloy box sections to support the sub-frame which carries the engine and transmission units, with their auxiliaries.

The rear section mates with the hind portion of the "punt" to enclose the wheel-arch, around which is a horse-shoe-shaped compartment for luggage. Integral with this section is the support for the driver's and passenger's seats and accommodation for one or two children.

The independent front suspension system, which has been tried and found successful in the high-speed Berkeley cars, embodies wishbones of unequal lengths carrying the king-pin brackets and steering trunnion-blocks. The spring elements are Armstrong hydraulically controlled units, unshrouded, and the wishbone pivots all work in Silentbloc bushes. Steering is by a Burman worm-and-nut unit, the three-piece track-rod and its connections also being provided with Silentbloc joints. At the rear, a single swinging arm, with overhung stub axle, works in Silentbloc bearings spaced 14-in. apart, rigidly located to the body structure and sprung by an Armstrong unit similar to those employed at the front. Steel tube, 2 in. in diameter and of 10g., is used for the arm, triangulation being by 1¼-in. tubes.

The air-cooled Excelsior engine, a development of the well-known "Talisman Twin" unit, develops 18 b.h.p. at 5,000 r.p.m., which gives the three-wheeler a power/weight ratio of approximately 60 b.h.p. per ton. The cylinder dimensions are 58 mm. by 62 mm. and the compression ratio 7.4:1. Mounted transversely between the Berkeley's front wheels, with the exhaust ports and cylinder heads exposed to an unobstructed airflow, the engine works under ideal conditions.

A single cable-controlled Amal carburetter is used. The short twin exhaust pipes lead into a large transverse expansion box and thence to an absorption-type silencer. Ignition is by two coils fed from the 12 v.

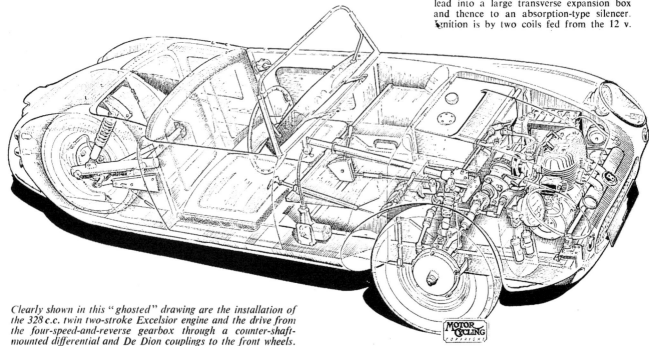

Clearly shown in this "ghosted" drawing are the installation of the 328 c.c. twin two-stroke Excelsior engine and the drive from the four-speed-and-reverse gearbox through a counter-shaft-mounted differential and De Dion couplings to the front wheels.

90 w. Siba " Dynastart " lighting and starting system. The 23 a.h. Exide car-type battery is accessibly mounted in the engine compartment, alongside the 3½-gal. gravity-feed petroil tank.

The engine drives a four-speed-and-reverse Albion gearbox via a ⅜-in. roller chain, fully enclosed in an oil bath. Forward gear ratios are 8.0, 11.1, 15.7 and 25.8:1; reverse is 27.5:1.

The seven-plate clutch has a shock-absorber centre. Transmission thence is by a short ½-in. chain to a countershaft running on double ball bearings carried in an alloy housing. On the countershaft is mounted the two-planet and four-star, straight-tooth-pinion differential, carried inside the boss of the final drive sprocket. From the differential run the short, stiff cardan shafts, each with an inboard and an outboard Hardy-Spicer mechanical universal joint, forming De Dion drive to the front wheels. Unsprung weight is thus kept to a minimum, which contributes considerably to the remarkable roadholding of the model.

The plastics body-cum-chassis of of the Berkeley has modern sports-car lines. Below is the roomy cockpit.

The 7-in.-diameter Girling brakes, their drums integral with the hubs, are hydraulically operated and interconnected; there is a separate parking control for that at the rear. The front brakes are of two-leading-shoe type. The 12-in. pressed-steel wheels, each mounted on five studs, are interchangeable and are fitted with 5.20-in. Michelin tyres. All hubs run on ball bearings; the front hubs are splined and nutted to their drive-shafts.

Controls are on car lines. The gears are operated by a short central lever working in a quadrant. The 16-in.-diameter steering wheel is of the modern two-spoke pattern. Hidden beneath the dash, but accessibly placed, is the air-control lever for the carburetter. The clutch pedal operates via a specially heavy cable.

A " divided " bench-type seat, 3 ft. 4½ in. wide, accommodates driver and passenger, the squab length, from front to back, being 1 ft. 7 in. and the height of the seat-back 2 in. greater. Upholstery is of Dunlopreen covered with Vynide. The safety-glass windscreen is of wrap-round type and its heavy, raked frame is supported by strong stays which also serve as grab handles.

Equipment includes twin windscreen wipers; dipping headlamps hidden behind streamlined, plastics-faced fairings; twin tail and stop lamps; direction-indicator winkers; a full-width parcel shelf beneath the dash, which carries, in addition to the normal switch gear, an A.C. 100 m.p.h. speedometer; and detachable sidescreens

and packaway hood in waterproof fabric. The floor covering is of Hardura plastic material.

Colour finishes available are red, light blue, British racing green and "Old English" white. Upholstery and body trimming can be had in red, black or brown.

Principal dimensions are: Wheelbase, 7 ft. 2 in.; track, 3 ft. 6¼ in.; overall length, 10 ft. 6 in.; width, 4 ft. 3 in.; height (hood erected), 3 ft. 11 in., (hood down), 3 ft. 5½ in.; ground clearance, 6 in.; dry weight, 6 cwt. 1 qr.

A short run in a prototype model substantiated the makers' claims for the performance of the Berkeley, with particular emphasis on roadholding and braking. It was found possible to put the machine into a three-wheel drift on a dry surface in perfect safety, while two-up it was stopped in 31 ft. from 30 m.p.h. on a level road.

In a subsequent issue we shall publish a full road test report on this welcome newcomer which promises to meet, at last, the demand for a three-wheeler providing sports-car motoring at motorcycle cost.

THE BERKELEY RANGE OF MODELS

Type	Engine	Brake Horse-Power	Model
Small two-seat	Royal Enfield 692 c.c. four-stroke	40	B95
" "	" " " " "	50	B105
Two/Occasional four-seat	" " " " "	40	Q95
Two/Occasional four-seat	" " " " "	50	Q105
Large two-seat	" " " " "	40	QB95
" "	" " " " "	50	QB105

SPECIFICATION COMMON TO ALL MODELS

BODY AND FRAME

Resin bonded moulded glass fibre with aluminium alloy bulkheads and cross members moulded in to form a single structure.

BRAKES

Seven inch Girling hydraulic: Front, two leading shoes; Rear, one trailing, one leading shoe. Adjustable handbrake operating rear shoes only.

SUSPENSION

All wheels independently sprung: Front by unequal wishbones with Girling or Armstrong coil spring and damper units; Rear by swing axles.

STEERING

Burman worm and nut steering box with three piece divided track rod and 16in. wheel.

WHEELS AND TYRES

Lightweight wheels with five-stud fixing fitted with 520 x 12 Michelin tyres. Spare wheel supplied.

ELECTRICAL EQUIPMENT

Twelve volt 32 amp. hr. battery. Dipping headlamps incorporating parking lights, foot dipping switch, two tail lamps incorporating hydraulically operated stop lights, two reflectors, dual arm electric windshield wiper, electric horn, flashing direction indicators.

CONTROLS AND CONTROL PANEL

Clutch, brake and accelerator pedals of pendant design. Gear change lever mounted centrally on floor, pistol type handbrake, ignition switch, panel switch, windscreen wiper switch, direction indicator switch.

SPECIFICATION OF THE ROYAL ENFIELD 692 c.c. ENGINE

TYPE '95'

Air-cooled vertical twin-cylinder o.h.v.

Bore: 70 m.m.

Stroke: 90 m.m.

Capacity: 692 c.c.

Output: 40 b.h.p. at 5,500 r.p.m.

Compression ratio: 7.25—1.

Carburation: One "Amal" carburettor.

Cylinder heads: Light alloy.

Pistons: Low expansion aluminium alloy.

Main Bearings: Heavy duty bearings are provided for the crankshaft, the driving side being ball and the timing side roller.

Crankshaft and Flywheel: The crankshaft is cast in one piece, integral with the central flywheel, from high quality meehanite cast iron, total weight 26 lb. The main journals are ground and hand lapped.

Valves: The inlet valves are machined from stampings of special Silicon-Chrome valve steel, and the exhaust valves are of austenitic steel.

Ignition: Lucas A.C. coil.

SPECIFICATION OF THE ROYAL ENFIELD 692 c.c. ENGINE

TYPE '105'

Air-cooled vertical twin-cylinder o.h.v.

Bore: 70 m.m.

Stroke: 90 m.m.

Capacity: 692 c.c.

Output: 50 b.h.p. at 6,250 r.p.m.

Compression ratio: 8—1.

Carburation: One "Amal" T.T. type carburettor.

Cylinder heads: Same as type '95'.

Pistons: Same as type '95'.

Main Bearings: Same as type '95'.

Crankshaft and Flywheel: Same as type '95'.

Valves: Same as type '95'.

Ignition: Same as type '95'.

INSTRUMENTS

Speedometer with ignition warning light, fuel gauge (r.p.m. indicator optional extra).

GENERAL EQUIPMENT

One-piece curved windscreen, "Vynide" upholstery, "Hardura" plastic carpets, driving mirror, hood, side screens, aluminium alloy wheel discs and imitation "knock-off" hubs. Set of tools.

VARIATIONS OF BASIC SPECIFICATION

B.95, B105, Q.95, Q.105, QB.95, QB.105

Electrical

All these models are fitted with a generator, starter and coil ignition equipment manufactured by Lucas.

Q.95 and Q.105

Body and Frame

Four seats (front seats are adjustable). Bonnet and air intake grille opens in one piece and hinged at the rear.

Wheels and Tyres

Spare wheel externally mounted at rear of car.

QB.95 and QB.105

Body and Frame

Four-seater body made to accommodate two front adjustable seats, and stowage for luggage and spare wheel in the rear of the car.

DIMENSIONS OF THE DIFFERENT MODELS

B.95 — B.105

Wheelbase	5' 10"	Overall width	4' 2"
Track front	3' 6½"	Overall height	3' 10" with hood
Track rear	3' 6"	Ground clearance	7"
Overall length	10' 5½"	Turning circle	28'
Dry weight approx. 7 cwt.			

Q.95, Q.105, QB.95, QB.105

Wheelbase	6' 6"	Overall width	4' 6"
Track front	3' 10½"	Overall height	3' 10" with hood
Track rear	3' 10"	Ground clearance	5½"
Overall length	11' 1½"	Turning circle	28'
Dry weight approx. 7½ cwt.			

Four-Stroke Berkeley

AT the Geneva Show a new Berkeley model—the B95—is being shown for the first time. Basically similar to the existing model which has a three-cylinder 492 c.c. Excelsior two-stroke engine, the new model has instead the Royal Enfield twin-cylinder, four-stroke unit of 692 c.c. This unit, which has been in use for seven years in motor-cycle sidecar outfits, has the paired cylinders mounted vertically. Drive to the front wheels is, as before, by chain through an Albion clutch and four-speed gear box of motor cycle type, to a chassis-mounted, spur-gear differential and universally jointed shafts. To accommodate the torque of this larger engine, the gear box is strengthened and double roller chains are used.

This engine-transmission unit, which can be lifted out complete for servicing, has a front mounting consisting of a tubular cross member with a rubber bush at each end. This bearer is roughly at mid-height of the engine mass to minimize vibration; the third mounting is at the final drive housing.

Iron cylinder castings are carried on a light alloy crankcase, in which a one-piece cast iron crankshaft with integral central flywheel is supported on ball and roller bearings. Plain bearings are employed for the big ends. Lubrication is by a dry sump system, with oil returned from the crankcase by a scavenge pump to a reservoir integral with the crankcase. Pushrods and rockers operated by twin camshafts actuate in-clined valves in light alloy cylinder heads, the combustion chambers being hemispherical. For installation in the Berkeley, a flywheel with toothed ring has been fitted to the left of the crankshaft and the primary chain case modified to incorporate a Lucas starter motor and Bendix pinion. A dynamo is belt-driven from a crankshaft pulley. Ignition is by coil and cartype contact breaker and distributor.

Claimed power output is 40 b.h.p. at 5,500 r.p.m.—an increase of 10 b.h.p. over the smaller two-stroke engine—but kerb weight is increased by only 40 lb. This gives the high figure of 101 b.h.p. per ton, based on kerb weight. Alternatively, the more powerful version of the Royal Enfield engine—the Constellation—may be fitted at extra cost. This develops a 50 b.h.p. at 6,250 r.p.m. on a compression ratio of 8 to 1, and the model is then known as the B105.

Frontal appearance of the glass-fibre body structure, reinforced by aluminium alloy bulkheads and steel cross members, has been changed. The bonnet line has been raised locally over the higher engine and a large rectangular grille admits cooling air direct to the cylinders. The bonnet is hinged at the front for access to the engine. Lucas P700 head lamps are now exposed instead of being sunk into the wings, and below them are the separate parking lights and flashing indicators. Overall length is 2½in greater.

Both versions of the Royal Enfield engine will later be installed in other models of the Berkeley range, namely, the occasional four-seater and a variant of this, in which the rear passenger space is to be reserved solely for luggage, and to be known as the large two-seater sports. Approximate prices, to be confirmed, are: Standard two-seater sports, total, including purchase tax, £659; two-four-seater and large two-seater sports, £714.

A brief drive in the two-seater prototype showed that acceleration is impressive and that, although one is aware of the twin cylinder motor cycle engine working hard, vibration is kept to a minimum by careful mounting. A higher performance and avoidance of the need to refuel with a petroil mixture should widen the appeal of this small sports car.

Front mounting for the vertical twin Royal Enfield engine is on a cross tube below the exhaust outlets. A starter is bolted to the front of the chain case

SPECIFICATION

ENGINE

Type	Royal Enfield Super Meteor
No. of cylinders ...	2 in line (transverse)
Bore and stroke...	70 x 90mm (2.75 x 3.54in)
Displacement ...	692 c.c. (42.2 cu in)
Valve position ...	o.h., pushrods, hemispherical combustion chambers
Compression ratio	7.25 to 1
Max. b.h.p. (gross)	40 at 5,500 r.p.m.
Max. b.m.e.p. ...	153 lb sq in at 4,000 r.p.m.
Max. torque ...	43 lb ft at 4,000 r.p.m.
Carburettor ...	Amal T.T. type
Fuel pump ...	S.U. electric
Fuel tank capacity	5 Imperial gallons (25 litres)
Oil tank capacity...	5 pints (2.84 litres)
Oil filter	Gauze strainer
Cooling system ...	Direct air cooled
Battery	12 volts, 32 ampere-hour

TRANSMISSION

Clutch	Albion multi-plate
Gear box... ...	Albion four speed and reverse, central quadrant change, dog engagement
Overall ratios ...	Top 4.31; 3rd 5.95; 2nd 8.62; 1st 13.7; reverse 14.05 to 1
Final drive ...	Duplex chain, ratio 2.32 to 1

CHASSIS

Brakes	Girling hydraulic, 2 L.S. front, L and T rear
Drum size ...	7in dia x 1¼in wide
Suspension: front	Unequal length wishbones, combined coil springs and telescopic dampers
rear	Single wishbones, combined coil springs and telescopic dampers
Wheels	Bolt-on disc
Tyres	5.20—12in Michelin
Steering	Burman worm and nut
Steering wheel ...	16in dia, two-spoke
Turns, lock to lock	2¼

DIMENSIONS
(Manufacturer's figures)

Wheelbase ...	5ft 10in (178 cm)
Track	front: 3ft 6½in (107.9 cm); rear: 3ft 6in (106.7 cm)
Overall length ...	10ft 5½in (319 cm)
Overall width ...	4ft 2in (127 cm)
Overall height ...	3ft 10in (117 cm) (hood up)
Ground clearance	7in (18 cm)
Turning circle ...	28ft (8.53m)
Kerb weight ...	7.9 cwt—887 lb approx (402 kg)

PERFORMANCE DATA

Top gear m.p.h. at 1,000 r.p.m.... ...	14.28
Torque lb ft per cu in engine capacity...	1.02
Brake surface area swept by linings ...	110 sq in

BERKELEY B·95

ONE OF THE FUNDAMENTAL TRUTHS that all sports car enthusiasts come to understand is that a car does not have to be terribly fast to be very interesting. In fact, most of us soon come to regard sheer speed as a secondary attribute, the qualities of handling and general sporting flavor being relatively more important. The subject of this test drives that point home very effectively, for

in the Berkeley B-95 very little actual speed seems like an awesome amount.

Two years ago, when we did a test of the first Berkeley sports car, everyone commented that if the 18.2-bhp 2-cylinder, 2-stroke engine were replaced with something more powerful, the car would be a real tiger. The idea apparently intrigued the makers as much as it did us, for

The coziest of cockpits.

The progressive-shift quadrant.

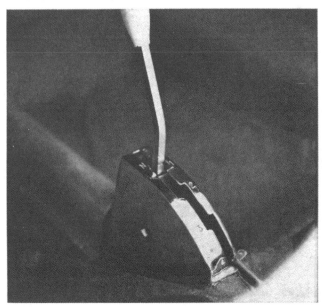

the model B-95 is propelled by a monstrous (compared with the total size of the car) 700-cc Enfield 2-cylinder, 4-stroke motorcycle engine. This unit, in the B-95, has a mild 40 bhp, but is also available with minor modifications that yield 10 bhp more. The Enfield engine is an impressive thing—all aluminum alloy and very business-like—and has really thunderous torque at low speed. Also, in spite of the long stroke and pushrod-operated valves, it will turn up to 6000 or more revolutions. In this connection, we would like to mention that it runs out of power well below the point of valve crash, which has the effect of discouraging the frivolous from using revolutions to the detriment of the engine.

The drive from the engine is very "motorcycle" in layout, with a double-row chain to the clutch and transmission, from which yet another chain carries the drive to the chassis-mounted final drive sprocket. The hub of the final drive sprocket contains the differential gears and from these originate the shafts that drive the front wheels. The second stage of the chain drive is exposed to the elements, but is lubricated by oil mist from an engine breather pipe.

The chassis is in unit with the body and is extremely unorthodox in its construction, being made entirely of fiberglass with a few aluminum or steel gussets at points where stresses are concentrated. All four wheels are independently suspended, on unequal length arms at the front and swing axles at the rear. The suspending medium is coil springs all around.

The body retains most of the contours from earlier models, but the various modifications needed to get the headlights up to a legal height and to enclose the tall, bulky engine have caused the appearance to suffer. In fact, the car is just a trifle grotesque from many angles. Even so, the quality of the finish is impressive in that there are none of the uneven surface ripples that have been such a problem to fiberglass fabricators.

With such absolutely minimal overall dimensions, it is scarcely surprising that the interior of the car is not overly roomy. The members of our test crew were each six feet tall and proportionately broad, and with both of them in the car there was just barely enough surplus room for the test equipment. Actually, two average-size people in the car will not be really cramped—but they certainly will be friendly.

Instrumentation is very complete and positioned so

The engine overhangs the front wheels.

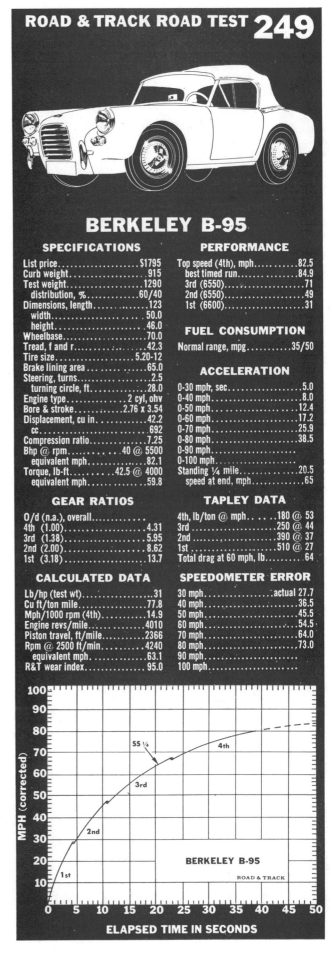

BERKELEY B-95

SPECIFICATIONS

List price	$1795
Curb weight	915
Test weight	1290
distribution, %	60/40
Dimensions, length	123
width	50.0
height	46.0
Wheelbase	70.0
Tread, f and r	42.3
Tire size	5.20-12
Brake lining area	65.0
Steering, turns	2.5
turning circle, ft	28.0
Engine type	2 cyl, ohv
Bore & stroke	2.76 x 3.54
Displacement, cu in	42.2
cc	692
Compression ratio	7.25
Bhp @ rpm	40 @ 5500
equivalent mph	82.1
Torque, lb-ft	42.5 @ 4000
equivalent mph	59.8

GEAR RATIOS

O/d (n.a.), overall	
4th (1.00)	4.31
3rd (1.38)	5.95
2nd (2.00)	8.62
1st (3.18)	13.7

CALCULATED DATA

Lb/hp (test wt)	31
Cu ft/ton mile	77.8
Mph/1000 rpm (4th)	14.9
Engine revs/mile	4010
Piston travel, ft/mile	2366
Rpm @ 2500 ft/min	4240
equivalent mph	63.1
R&T wear index	95.0

PERFORMANCE

Top speed (4th), mph	82.5
best timed run	84.9
3rd (6550)	71
2nd (6550)	49
1st (6600)	31

FUEL CONSUMPTION

Normal range, mpg	35/50

ACCELERATION

0-30 mph, sec	5.0
0-40 mph	8.0
0-50 mph	12.4
0-60 mph	17.2
0-70 mph	25.9
0-80 mph	38.5
0-90 mph	
0-100 mph	
Standing ¼ mile	20.5
speed at end, mph	65

TAPLEY DATA

4th, lb/ton @ mph	180 @ 53
3rd	250 @ 44
2nd	390 @ 37
1st	510 @ 27
Total drag at 60 mph, lb	64

SPEEDOMETER ERROR

30 mph	actual 27.7
40 mph	36.5
50 mph	45.5
60 mph	54.5
70 mph	64.0
80 mph	73.0
90 mph	
100 mph	

Really flying! The high speed (?) run.

that it can be read with a minimum of neck-craning—though in all truth it must be said that it would be almost impossible to place the instruments any place *but* near the driver. The controls are also well located, albeit grouped a bit closely, and the only complaint we have concerns the gearshift lever. As the gearbox is positioned ahead of the front wheels, there is a remote shift device—which consists of a long rod, connecting the transmission and the shift lever. The shift pattern is most peculiar, all positions being located progressively along a notched quadrant—not unlike the arrangement used by Harley-Davidson for many years. The gears are non-synchronized, but as the transmission runs at less than engine speed, extremely fast snap shifts can be made—just as with a motorcycle. Some practice is required before one becomes proficient at making fast shifts—either up or down—and we feel that it would have been better if the complete motorcycle-type gearchange had been used. Shifting would have then become a simple matter of tugging the lever back to change up, and pushing forward to change down—or vice versa.

Driving the Berkeley, especially "at speed," is an experience never to be forgotten. One sits less than 10 inches above the road surface and the bounding, choppy ride, combined with the booming exhaust note, lends a

sporting air that we had thought irrevocably lost to the past. Although this car is entirely unlike any pre-war sports car, it nonetheless manages to *feel* just like one. The first big point of similarity is the manner in which the chassis appears to flex as the car flails down the road. It might be mentioned here that due to a certain "scale" effect, every little bump and ripple in a road surface takes on enormous proportions. The Berkeley doesn't ride badly, except over very bad roads, but on any uneven surfaces at near-maximum speeds it begins to feel very light—which it actually is. During our high-speed runs the car was quite stable—in spite of a brisk side-wind—but still felt as though it were just flitting from one bump to the crest of the next.

The overall performance of the B-95 was somewhat puzzling, as it proved to be slightly better in acceleration than we had anticipated—but not nearly so fast at the top end. According to the manufacturer, the Berkeley should be capable of nearly 100 mph, and our best run was some 15 mph short of that. However, our test car's engine was in rather ragged condition—due to 10,000 miles of use as a "demonstrator." We think that a B-95 in peak condition might go better—but we're not altogether sure that we would want to drive it *too* much faster. A prototype version of the 50 bhp Berkeley B-105 has actually been timed at speeds exceeding 100 mph, a feat which we suspect required considerable courage.

Taken as a whole, the Berkeley B-95 is not so much a *good* car as it is a *fun* car. Tearing around in such an absurd vehicle may not be dignified or practical, but it certainly is a delightful way to spend a sunny afternoon.

Actually, the best use for the car that occurs to us would be as a true sports/racing car. The B-95 could be a real terror in its competition class and would serve as a sporting runabout away from the race course. It is not the car for just everyone, particularly when driven with vigor, as it is stable only so long as the power is on. The Berkeley has a pronounced tendency to weave and dodge when one's foot is lifted suddenly from the throttle, which is a trifle unsettling. And, even worse, it is possible to almost lose control if the brakes are applied hard at high speeds. One would therefore be well advised to use discretion until complete familiarity with this machine is achieved. Still, for the person who appreciates a little character and spirit, even at the expense of practicality, the Berkeley B-95 is an intriguing automobile. Our entire staff turned out to drive the car and, even though most aware of its deficiencies, thoroughly enjoyed the experience.

This view gives scant evidence of the car's small size.

Air cooling—requires a lot of air.

THE 1960 BERKELEY

At its recent premier showing in Hollywood, the diminutive but potent Berkeley model B-95 sports roadster captured a most unusual measure of attention in a community that is just a little blase when it comes to sports cars.

BABY *from Britain* BOMB

The reasons are quite obvious, for the builders of this British import lay claim to a sports car that will reach 100 mph and is priced at less than $1800! Other rather amazing claims are a 0-to-60 mph acceleration time of 15 seconds and fuel consumption of 45 mpg.

Under the hood of the B-95 is a two-cylinder, air-cooled, Royal Enfield engine displacing 692 cc and delivering 40 bhp at 5500 rpm. This hot little mill has push rod actuated overhead valves and runs at a compression ratio of 7.25 to 1. The drive to the front wheels is through a multi-plate clutch and four-speed.

Constructed around a 70-inch wheelbase, the body and frame are an integral unit of molded fiberglass, with aluminum alloy bulkheads and cross-members molded in to form a single structure. An outstanding feature of this construction is the full belly pan which serves to stiffen and streamline the car. All four wheels are independently suspended utilizing combined coil springs and shock absorbers. **END**

Air-cooled, two-cylinder OHV engine delivers 100 mph.

Back to front drive, and test chief Blain celebrates by bending tiny Berkeley racer through SCW's trial turn without fuss yet very, very fast. Car is so light Michelin X tyres (inflated to racing pressures) hardly distort. Pic 1 demonstrates B105's roll-free turning capabilities, although wheels assume odd angles due to cunning suspension design. By Pic 2 tail has broken and car is sliding bodily sideways, still thoroughly under control. Pic 3 points to absence of drama as fast, stable, highly controll-able Berkeley accelerates out.

DOUG BLAIN DRIVES THE

BEWILDERIN

NEVER before can a car so tiny so have caught Australian enthusiasts' imagination as Berkeley's pert, aggressive B105 has done. Ever since our first brief notes on the new, big-engine light-weight appeared in December of last year we've been favoured with a steady stream of letters demanding price, distribution and above all *performance* details. How does the thing go? the letters kept asking. Can it really see off an MGA? Can it really tip the ton? Can it really zip through corners faster than practically anything else around?

We won't be cruel. We haven't the heart to keep you guessing for six whole pages. Right here and now let's place it on record that the answer to almost all your questions is a straight yes.

Racing men have known for decades that the one incontestable way to extract extra urge from any car is to add cubic inches. Family car makers, by dint of grudging and much-fanfared four and five percent annual litreage increases, have been at it since the first automobile scared the last horse back into the roadless wastes where he belonged. Sports car builders, by tradition, are bolder. Only last year MG added 100 cc to their A-type roadster donk. Three years before they'd whacked on a cool 200-odd, or almost 20 percent. People thought Austin Healey were equally bold when they boosted the 100-Six to 3000 cc recently.

Big they may be, but all these increases pale to insignificance in the light of Berkeley's decision to heap nearly 700 cc into a frame

they planned for 300! Add to that the B105's 104 cwt laden weight figure and you'll begin to realise why this little demon moves so very fast.

Yet it's all very well to go generalising about big joints in little dishes. Even though doubling engine size may be a sure short cut to relatively reliable high performance, the process can bring trouble in other departments. Dragsters here at home, and particularly in the US, are a case in point. Dragment or dragbugs, or whatever they're called, are much given to applying the beef-or-bust technique to the business of power extraction. Such types have been known to squeeze two and even three huge hairy V-8s into their lumpy-looking projectiles in search of extra jump. They get it (given suitable tyres and transmissions), but start a dragster in a typical circuit race and it will lose no time ramming our point right home — probably in a devastating first-corner crash. The truth is that thirst for sheer output in cars like that has left the sciences of roadholding, suspension and braking very much on the outer. That, in the dragster world, is perfectly acceptible. But what happens when you apply drag techniques to the world's smallest true production sports car chassis? Is the Berkeley B105 just another highly improbable two-lap terror?

Taking the metaphor for a moment at its face value, no. In almost 600 solid miles of racing, our actual test car has established for itself an honour roll that takes some laughing off. The car in question is somewhat unique. Pre-

pared for house-sponsored racing by Australia-wide franchise holders Auto Imports Pty Ltd., of Sydney, the car we tested naturally carries an item or two of extra equipment. But here's the rub. Not only has absolutely nothing apart from the windscreen been either removed or replaced, but the engine has come through without a single deviation from stock. In that light the little car's trail of triumphs over almost innumerable cars up to five and six times its size becomes more than remarkable. Who, for instance, could have failed to go away impressed after watching Auto Imports manager Paul Samuels circulate the B105 at Bathurst ahead of more than half its open opposition, including everything from a Twin Cam MG to a blown Sprite?

A record like that indicates something more than just sheer power. After all, the B105's power-weight ratio (see data panel) isn't so impressive as to let it walk away from such opposition without benefit of not just equal, but *better* roadholding qualities. Those we will testify to, after having seen Samuels at work on Murray's Corner at Bathurst and particularly after having tried for ourselves in SCW's celebrated test corner.

Indeed acceleration and cornering ability are the tiny, relatively pricey Berkeley's twin towers of strength. In less important things its superiority is doubtful.

For a start, the B105 looks what it is — a magnificent basic design full of cunning but controversial afterthoughts. Its basic body lines are beautiful in the true sense. No excess ornament, no unnecessary

Step this way for vintage motoring *almost* a la mode.

BERKELEY B105 LE MANS

saying we thought the original two-stroke Berkeley one of the most satisfying cars, aesthetically, we had seen. The B105 is not aesthetically satisfying. Its front has been butchered to make way for a comparatively huge four-stroke, air-cooled Royal Enfield Constellation vertical twin, all of which is located forward of the front wheel centreline. Yet all things considered, Berkeley has done a praiseworthy job getting the tall, top-heavy Enfield into the scheme of things at all. And even though the resultant styling exercise, with its big square grille, its gaping rear-facing air outlet slot, its cramped lighting arrangements and its bastard bumpers is somewhat regrettable from a purist point of view, at least it looks neat and relatively smart. We can think of far more ugly sports cars, one of which happens to be the Berkeley's nearest market opponent.

Inside, things are rather more happy. Driver and passenger sit comfortably and not too close in recesses on a single seat that actually (for reasons of space) forms part of the coachwork. Backrest and cushion are made from strips of special rubber slung across the car, supported at three points and rather sparsely padded. The result is seating which offers little resilience, but which is comfortable nevertheless because it is properly shaped to support most sizes in human anatomy at all the right spots. Sole drawback is that the arrangement offers no adjustment for leg or arm length. We can't speak for the compacts, but as a tester of some physical length we found ourselves quite admirably, if not ideally, catered for.

Leg and elbow room was adequate. The small, two-spoke black plastic wheel came about as close as an MGA's — a state of

At the head of it all, husky Enfield Constellation answers many an unvoiced query.

affairs which we consider not to be ideal, yet which allows reasonably free arm movement if you keep your hands at a quarter to three. With the Berkeley's quick steering, big arm sweeps aren't often necessary anyway. The three pedals are too small, too slippery and too closely grouped, yet their relative placing makes heel-and-toe changes possible and leaves adequate room for off-clutch resting.

Berkeleys have long used a highly efficient, almost unique gearchange system. The instrument of change itself is a small plated lever against the seat in the middle of the neatly rubber-covered cockpit floor. The lever moves in a sort of fore-and-aft gate. Positions for the gears are easy to find because the gate, instead of being a single long slot, is off-centre, changing sides at each change point. In practice that means that to change cogs you move the lever either forward or back (depending on whether you're changing down or up) until it comes to the end of that particular plane of the slot. To line up for the next change spring loading moves the lever across, from where you just proceed as before. The lever connects to a special constant mesh four-speed Albion gearbox mounted in unit with and chain-driven from the engine, driving to the front wheels through a limited-slip differential and jointed half-shafts. The ar-rangement gives clean, simple and extremely quick changing through the whole range. It is possible to double-clutch for downward swaps, but personally we doubt that there's any necessity for it. The lever is well placed and crisp of feel.

A full tray of instruments faces the driver, albeit from a central grouping. Big speedometer and tachometer dials are ideally calibrated, the latter in units of 100 to 7000 rpm (all of which seems to be legitimately usable, since there is no red line). Minor dials, also neatly marked in white on black, indicate battery charge and fuel level. The test car had an extra oil pressure gauge, available optionally. Another car we saw on the showroom floor had no tachometer, but we were told that was a factory mistake. All Berkeleys now sold in Australia are supposed to have them.

The pleasant-to-hold wheel carries an enamel B motif in red and white. The same badge is repeated on the car's nose and on each of the alloy knock-off screws that secure slotted aluminium rim-discs for the spider-type integral brake drums and road wheels. The steering wheel badge does not operate a horn. Instead, the button is on the dash within finger's reach of the rim. An identical button for the dynastart is just the other side of the ignition key, three inches or so away — not a good idea on paper, although in practice we had no trouble telling them apart. Other cockpit equipment on the test car included an all-enveloping perspex windshield for the driver only; a clip-on fibre tonneau cover; an alloy headrest, padded and trimmed in vinyl fabric; twin dash-top rear view mirrors. It is this equipment plus a set of bonnet-top louvres in aluminium that distinguishes the Le Mans model (marketed only in Australia and an Auto Imports exclusive) from the normal B 105. Extra cost for the furnishings is £80-odd extra, but for that you get more than glamour. The perspex screen lowers frontal area enough to let the Berkeley's Enfield engine push it over 100 mph on occasion, although at inadvisable revolutions 100 mph — we know not why — is still considered something of a magical figure.

Behind the cockpit is space either for a child or for limited luggage. A fibre cover shields the space, although it can be diced when the neat black fabric hood is up (normal B 105 only). To get kids in behind, the spare wheel must be restowed on a commodious shelf under the dash. Otherwise the shelf serves as extra baggage space. Both doors have pockets for oddments.

Even with all these odd spots of stowage, luggage placement is a big problem in the Berkeley. A luggage rack of sorts is, we think, an essential option.

The compact, nicely finished Constellation engine fits in up front with plenty of space left over for working. Since the engine is located forward of the front

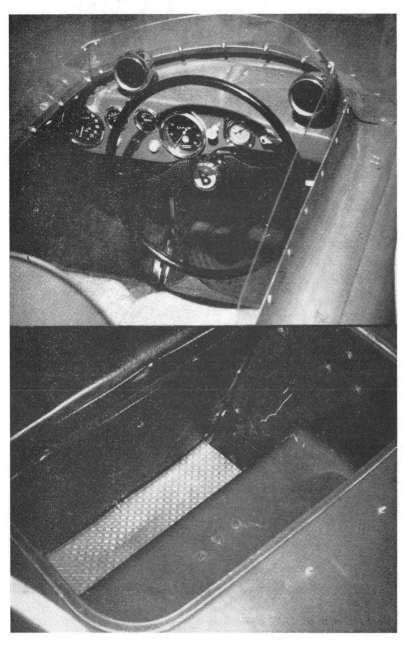

Operations centre in Le Mans variant leaves driver isolated, exposed but well catered for. LOWER: Yep, brats too! But luggage must share strictly limited space.

wheel centreline, auxilliaries share an airy area at the back of the spacious bay with the battery and electrical gear. The fuel tank, scuttle-mounted in the first two-stroke Berkeleys, now lives in the tail. The entire engine-transmission-final drive set up removes easily for major attention.

Starting the Berkeley is no problem. A normal Bendix-type electric motor engages a modest auxiliary flywheel and sets, things off. The test car had no choke control (disconnected for racing), so early-morning starts meant getting out and putting a hand over the intake for the single Amal carburettor. Regular examples do have a dash-mounted button control.

We spent some time reacquainting ourselves with the Albion constant-mesh gearbox and multiple clutch. Finding first slot is sometimes a trifle tricky, and the clutch shows sudden death inclinations, but once you master the set-up you're king in any situation. As with any inherently well-balanced clutch mechanism, practice is the only requirement for perfect changing. The Berkeley arrangement shares plenty with many better-class vintage movements; like them, it refuses to slip in any circumstance.

Forward ratios are all on the high side, and close at that, but since the final drive incorporates quite a sizeable stepdown you end up with an extremely low top gear mph/1000 figure at 14.3. The net result is, a very pleasant box of cogs. Top gear, because of the Enfield's one firing impulse per revolution and its high-up torque characteristics, gives rise to a misleading and at first baffling idea that it is an overdrive. In fact it is far from it, but the box is best treated that way. Third gear has a peak high enough to allow continuous cruising in steep or twisting country, thanks to the B 105's generous, rev limit.

The Berkeley is one of those sports cars that just loves to work hard. It is common practice to put 65000 on the clock regularly in the intermediates, and the compact pushrod engine will willingly go higher, beyond the red line. All the right noises, accompany the process. The exhaust barks joyously out behind, losing itself in a surge of sound from the valve gear. In fact the B 105 is no car for the man who can't take his, motoring on the rocks. The engine rocker gear lives right out in the air stream — actually visible through a huge bonnet-top outlet slot both to driver and to passenger. Needless to say the noise at high revolutions is loud indeed. On top of that there's a continuous motor-cycle vibration when the engine is going, although it is seldom unpleasantly obtrusive except at a point just above idling speed (600 rpm).

To any self-respecting enthusiast all that is part of the fun. The churn of threshing valve gear, the howl of a barely restricted exhaust, the rush of an 80 mph gale — such factors are wine to him.

Regular Berkeley B95 and B105 models carry no front louvres, look far cleaner.

BEWILDERING BERKELEY B105 LE MANS

Most other aspects of the Berkeley's performance fit the formula. Knife-sharp steering, quite unaffected by the terrific weight concentration on the front wheels, transmits an intimate knowledge of road conditions without reacting unduly to bumps. The steering shows good self-centreing. It is light and quick always. Even at parking speeds one hand is plenty.

Brakes. The Berkeley's tremendous lining area provides theoretical retardation second to none. The test car, race-weary in that department, had lost some of the keen edge from its stopping efficiency, but even so its brakes impressed us as adequate. Experience of a new B 105 some time ago showed that results normally are spectacular.

The Berkeley is driven from its front wheels. Independent rear suspension by coils and big single semi-wishbones supports the tail.

How can a car with all its weight in front and a tail that can be lifted easily by one man be expected to handle at sports car speeds in corners? People will tell you ridiculous things about lightweight cars. Time and again you can hear it said that such-and-such a car needs sand in the boot before it will handle. By and large such claims are monstrous. A tiny, light car can be made to handle just as well as a big, heavy one provided tyre contact area and centre of gravity are proportionate. Admittedly bumps and wet roads can throw things out, because bumps of a given size get proportionately more forbidding as wheels and weights decrease, and a tyre that is resilent enough to soak up big bumps on a small wheel may not have a big enough load concentration to penetrate the greasy film that coats any road in the wet. Paul Samuels tells us that on occasion a trunkful of gravel has made several seconds' worth of difference to his wet-weather lap times. But remember that a race track is far more slippery on a wet day than any highway is likely to be. A downpour during our test convinced us that the Berkeley's handling in main road circumstances stays almost equally excellent, wet or dry.

The predominant characteristic is, of course, understeer. Final oversteer can be counted on in most extreme situations, although it takes a lot of provoking. Usually the technique is to approach a given corner well on the high side of your usual speed in literally *any* sports car and — just hold it all the way through! The Berkeley does the rest, scudding through as if it were painted on the road. Razor-slotted Michelin Xs clench their way in and out again with barely a moan. Front wheels point rigidly to the inside verge while the back ones, knock-kneed under deflection, follow meekly along behind.

Put everything you have into it and the process stays much the same, except that by the time

---

TECHNICAL DETAILS:

PERFORMANCE

TOP SPEED:

Two-way average	91.9
Fastest one way	93.0
Theoretical (at 6500 rpm)	92.95

ACCELERATION:

(Test limit 6500rpm)

Through Gears:

(Times in parentheses from graph, not direct)

0-30 mph	NA	(2.8 sec)
0-40 mph	NA	(5.5)
0-50 mph	NA	(9.0)
0-60 mph		16.0
0-70 mph		29.8
0-80 mph		NA
Standing quarter-mile		best, 19.2 sec
		average, 19.7 sec
Speed at end of quarter		63 mph
Best ascent Foley's Hill		NA

MAXIMUM SPEED IN GEARS:

(at 6500 rpm)

I	30 mph
II	47 mph
III	67 mph

SPEEDOMETER ERROR:

NA [NOTE: test car's speedometer inoperative; spot check of tachometer for acceleration runs showed slight pessimism: 3000 rpm (indicated) = 3025 (actual)].

TAPLEY DATA:

Maximum pull in gears:

I	600lb ton at 24 mph
II	500lb ton at 25 mph
III	275lb ton at 23 mph
IV	220lb ton at 29 mph

BRAKING:

Average retardation at maximum pressure: NA (see text)

CALCULATED DATA:

Weight as tested (2 men) cwt	10.25
Max bhp (gross only)	50
Max torque (gross only)	45
Lb/hp (gross laden)	22.8
Mph/1000 rpm top gear	14.3
Mph at 2,500 ft/min piston speed top gear	60.5
Cub. cm/lb ft torque	15.38
Bhp/litre	72.5
Bhp/ton as tested	97.5
Brake lining area/ton as tested	120.25
Piston speed at max. bhp, fpm	3768

you're through you find yourself with just a shade of opposite lock in hand, wondering where the corner went. The throttle, we need hardly add, is your best friend in any such situation with a front drive car. The Berkeley obeys every rule. It is one of the best-handling sports cars we have yet driven, front *or* rear wheel drive.

Now for our one big quarrel. The B 105's suspension is, to put it mildly, lousy. Oh sure, the geometry is fine. If it were not, the car wouldn't handle. But a bump of any proportion puts the poor little Berkeley to such tremendous embarrassment that you wonder how in hell the factory ever had the temerity to let such a hopelessly under-sprung car through its gates. Our test car had its tyres inflated to racing level and its shockers were about done anyway, but even so the crashes that emanated from that heavily-laden front end each time we let a wheel stray into a pothole made us realise that no amount of adjustment would compensate either for springing that is far too soft or for damping

that is just plain inadequate. We don't want this to put you off buying a Berkeley: any garageman could beef up the suspension to make it really good by recalculating the spring rates and fitting fatter shockers. But we do think the factory should have thought of it first . . .

Finally, a word about the data panel. Seldom have we conducted a test against such hopeless odds. It was raining steadily. The Berkeley's speedometer cable had packed up. A hefty sidewind was lashing water across the strip. For these reasons all acceleration times are subject to error because of wheelspin, and the 0-50 and 0-60 times to further irregularity because they had to be taken against the tachometer. Other figures were out of the question. Remember that times for the normal B 105 should correspond exactly, except that top speed would suffer from the increased resistance set up by a full width windscreen as against that of a six-inch plastic shield and two very wet human heads. As it was, we

failed to record 100mph both ways in level flight, although we did see its equivalent on occasion during the test period The speed quoted in the table represents maximum permissible sustained revs, anyway — which isn't bad.

The best way to sum up the Berkeley is to say it is a true sports car in the hairy tradition of the old two-cylinder Morgan three-wheeler, the chain-gang Frazer-Nash, the vintage GN and a few others. More than any other automobile within thousands of pounds of its price, it is capable of generating almost limitless driving enjoyment. There is no need to make allowances for its size in terms of sheer performance; it will out-accelerate, outcorner and out-stop any competitor with ease. True, the B 105 has its faults. But when you come to think of it most of them can be translated, according to your sense of values, into distinct advantages.

We don't say the Berkeley will become a volume seller, but we're ready to listen to anyone who says it ought to be.   #

B E R K E L E Y   B 1 0 5   L E   M A N S

S P E C I F I C A T I O N S

PRICE:
£1095 including tax (Le Mans modifications, £80 extra)
ENGINE:
Type: Vertical twin, air-cooled.
Valves: Pushrod overhead.
Cubic Capacity: 692cc.
Bore & Stroke: 70 mm x 90 mm.
Piston Area: 11.9 sq. in.
Compression Ratio: 8.0 to 1.
Carburettors: Single Amal 10 TT9.
Fuel Pump: SU electric.
Max. Power: 50 bhp (gross) at 6250 rpm.
Max. torque: 45lb at 5500 rpm.

CHASSIS:
Type: Unit glass fibre and aluminium body/chassis.
Wheelbase .... 5ft. 10in.
Track, front .... 3ft. 6.25 in.
Track, rear .... 3ft. 6in.
Suspension, front .... Single wishbones, coil-shocker units
rear .... Coil, divided axle
Shock absorbers .... integral piston, Armstrong and Girling
Steering .... Burman worm and nut; turns, 2.0
Brakes: type .... Girling drum; 7 in front and rear
operation .... hydraulic   lining area .... 65 sq. in.
Clutch .... Albion multiple, 5.25 in.

GEAR RATIOS:

I	13. 7 to 1	III	5.95 to 1
II	8.62 to 1	IV	4.31 to 1
		Final Drive	2.23 to 1

GENERAL:
Length overall .... 10 ft 5.5 in.
Width .... 4 ft 2 in.
Height (to screentop) .... 3 ft 7.5 in.
Hood erection time (2 men) .... Not fitted to Le Mans
Test weather: Wet, strong side wind across strip.
All test runs made on bitumen-bonded gravel road with driver and one passenger aboard. All times averaged from several runs in opposite directions, using where applicable a corrected tachometer only.

THE EDITOR LIKED:	AND DISLIKED:
● **performance**	● **suspension**
● **roadholding**	● **styling**
● **steering**	● **luggage space**
● **brakes**	● **engine characteristics**
● **driving position**	● **wear factor**
● **accessibility**	● **price**
● **economy**	
● **cockpit layout**	
● **trim**	

BERKELEY BANDIT

▶ **NEW CAR FOR 1961**

FOR ANNOUNCEMENT of their new two-seater sports car, Berkeley of Biggleswade could not have chosen a better time. In launching one of the two completely new cars of the Show, the company focus attention on a move which takes them right out of the miniature car class and puts them into competition with the big names in the industry.

Firmly established as caravan makers, Berkeley's venture into the field of car manufacture was a move to underpin their future with an alternative product. Their experience with the small QB95 car was an excellent apprenticeship in this sphere, proving that they have the necessary commercial and engineering background to launch and market a car.

Called the Bandit, the new car can be considered a natural development, and at a price, with purchase tax, of a fraction under £800, including disc brakes at the front and all-round independent suspension, it merits careful consideration.

Commercial acumen was shown again in choosing an acknowledged designer, this time John Tojeiro, as consultant in the project. Tojeiro has broken away completely from the firm's previous practice, without throwing away their vast experience in glass-fibre techniques, by opting for a freestanding steel chassis and

rear wheel drive. Engine location remains at the front. It was also apparent that motorcycle units could not be considered and a Ford 105E engine-gearbox unit in standard tune was chosen as the prime mover. Even the swing axle rear end is basically Ford, and no doubt the wholesale use of these reliable and easily serviced components will be an important sales factor.

The foundation of the car is basically a square frame made from light-gauge steel channel and two welded-up box sections, which do double duty as body sills. At the forward end a strong scuttle structure is formed by two "foot-boxes," joined together top and bottom. Fabricated extensions pick up with the upper end of the MacPherson front suspension pillars and provide engine and radius arm mountings.

Rear cross members of the frame are two medium-diameter tubes; these carry, amidships, longitudinal flat plates which cradle the rubber-mounted final drive. Flanges at their vertical extremities carry bosses for the inboard pivots of the swing axle radius arms. To complete the assembly, vertical channel members, welded to the sills, form solid supports for door hinges and locks, experience with glass-fibre door pillars having shown that the flexibility of the material is too great.

The MacPherson-type front suspension is of Berkeley manufacture, utilizing an Armstrong coil and damper strut pivoting at its lower end in a ball joint. Round section steel rods are used for the lower transverse and radius arms, which are pivoted at their inner ends on rubber bushes. Alford and Alder rack and pinion steering is mounted forward of the wheel centre line. Girling disc brakes of 8in. dia. complete the assembly.

Construction of the swinging axle layout at the rear is typical of the realistic Berkeley approach to economic low-volume production. The basis is a normal 105E axle, bought complete from

Left: There are no afterthoughts in the rear lighting layout.   Right: Unusual in this class of car is the opening luggage boot

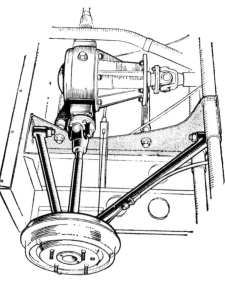

Two tubular radius arms, swinging about the U-joint centreline, locate the rear wheels

which has to be stowed away in an open car. It is wide enough to hold a passport. Deep door pockets with elastic tops provide space for maps, there is a parcel shelf for oddments, and carpet lines the stowage space behind the seats.

Safety has been carefully considered, a thick padded roll stretching the whole width of the facia, with the speedometer and optional rev. counter inset in a panel in front of the driver. Switches, fuel gauge and ammeter are set in a console-type panel below the facia. The optional recirculating heater is located behind this panel. There are grab handles on the tunnel, and incorporated with the windscreen supports.

Pendant-type pedals make heel-and-toe action a problem, lessened by the excellent synchromesh on the Ford gearbox, which is operated by a short and very well-placed lever. The handbrake lies in a rather too horizontal position between the driver's seat and the propeller shaft tunnel.

It was possible to obtain a brief impression of the handling of the car in the country lanes around Biggleswade and general road behaviour was quite in keeping with the specification. Weight distribution is almost 50-50, and with the low centre of gravity and commendably light steering it was possible to fling the car through fast corners at the limit of tyre adhesion without roll. There was none of the awkwardness of control which sometimes goes with a sports car and one was immediately at home with the car.

Despite a rather soft action the disc brakes pulled the car up absolutely square in a very short distance. In a village where drain-laying was in progress it was possible to ascertain that the suspension gave a good ride over very uneven surfaces, albeit with some noise.

Future plans for the car include conventional and "fast back" hardtops, while there is room for fitting an FWA Coventry-Climax engine. The car will sell for £562 17s (basic), total with tax £798 10s.

Dagenham. This is first stripped, the axle tubes are cut off close to the differential housing and flanges are welded on to the apertures to carry outrigged bearing and oil seal housings. Next the hub bearing housings are cut from the axle tubes and the swing axle radius arms welded to them; at the same time the oil seals are reversed to act as grease retainers. Finally the halfshafts are cut and a Hardy Spicer universal joint inserted. Rear brakes are the standard 8in. Anglia 105E drum type.

While impregnated glass-fibre is a more expensive material than steel, and therefore only justified for relatively small production, the production cost is all the time changing in favour of this material thanks to the constantly falling price of resins. Berkeley, therefore, do not envisage steel construction in the future.

An important factor is the size, for with an overall length of almost 12ft, all suggestion of a miniature is lost; the occupants sit well down in the car behind the curved, fixed windscreen.

Upholstery is carried out in leather-cloth of good quality, the seats adjusting to give plenty of leg-room for tall people. Between the seats a padded armrest has a lockable lid for the small impedimenta

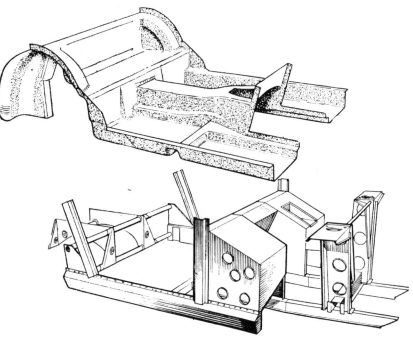

The complex sheet steel chassis frame is braced by the glass fibre floor which is riveted to it

SPECIFICATION

ENGINE

No. of cylinders	...	4 in line
Bore and stroke	...	80·96 x 48·41 mm (3·19 x 1·91in.)
Displacement	...	997 c.c. (60·84 cu. in.)
Valve position	...	Overhead
Compression ratio	...	8·9 to 1
Max. b.h.p. (gross)	...	41 at 5,000 r.p.m.
Max. b.h.p. (net)	...	39 at 5,000 r.p.m.
Max. b.m.e.p.	...	130 p.s.i. at 2,700 r.p.m.
Max. torque	...	52lb/ft. at 2,700 r.p.m.
Carburettor	...	Solex
Fuel pump	...	A.C. mechanical
Tank capacity	...	7 Imperial gallons (31·8 litres)
Sump capacity	...	4 pints (2·3 litres)
Oil filter	...	Cartridge (type A.C.21)
Cooling system	...	Pressurised, pump, fan and thermostat.
Battery	...	12 volt 38 amp. hr.

TRANSMISSION

Clutch	...	Single, dry plate
Gearbox	...	Four speeds, central gear lever
Overall gear ratios	...	Top 4·12; 3rd 5·83; 2nd 9·89; 1st 16·99; reverse 22·29
Final drive	...	Hypoid, ratio 4·125 to 1

CHASSIS

Brakes	...	F. Girling disc brakes; R. Girling internal expanding
Brake size	...	F. 8in. disc; R, 8 x 1¼in.
Suspension	...	F, Independent MacPherson type, coil springs. R, Independent swing axles, coil springs
Dampers	...	Armstrong telescopic
Wheels	...	Pressed disc
Tyre size	...	5·60 x 13in.
Steering	...	Rack and pinion
Steering wheel	...	Wood rimmed. 15in. diameter
Turns lock to lock	...	3·5

DIMENSIONS (Manufacturer's figures)

Wheelbase	...	6ft. 10in. (208 cm.)
Track	...	3ft. 10in. (117 cm.)
Overall length	...	11ft. 11·12in. (363 cm.)
Overall width	...	4ft. 6·62in. (139 cm.)
Overall height	...	3ft 8in. (112 cm.)
Ground clearance	...	5in. (12·7 cm.)
Turning circle	...	29ft (8.83 m.)
Kerb weight	...	1,450 lb—13 cwt (657 Kg.) (approximately)

PERFORMANCE DATA

Top gear m.p.h. at 1,000 r.p.m.	...	15·7
Torque lb ft per cu. in. engine capacity	...	0·865
Weight distribution	...	F. 51 per cent; R. 49 per cent.

BERKELEY BANDIT

IF AT FIRST THERE SEEMS to be something vaguely familiar about the looks of the brand new Berkeley, the Bandit, don't let appearances deceive you—the Bandit is like no other sports car marketed in England, and resembles earlier models only in its fiberglass body material.

The Bandit made its debut at the London Motor Show, but we were able to have a sneak preview about two weeks before it was revealed. When we first saw the white car parked well away from the road at the Biggleswade, Bedfordshire, factory, we thought that it looked like a Corvette from the rear. Then, from the front, it suggested a Renault Floride. However, managing director of Berkeley cars Charles Panter said he had not yet seen a Floride when design of the Bandit started about a year ago.

The car has rather deceptive lines, as have the older versions, and at first looks as if it is at least the size of an MG-A. On further inspection it becomes clear that it is nearer the Sprite in size, and it becomes apparent that the main sell for the Bandit will be toward people who had a Sprite in mind, but would like a little extra, for a little more money.

Strictly a 2-seater, the car is very snug. Neither driver nor passenger are cramped, however, and both sit in sub-stantial leather-covered bucket seats confronted by a deep, padded, leather-covered instrument panel. Red was used for the interior color of the prototype, and the whole thing was quite plush.

In the prototype, a handy sized 100-mph speedometer and 6000-rpm rev counter were placed in a nacelle in front of the driver, but the tachometer is to be an optional extra on the production car. Other instruments, the fuel gauge and ammeter, are placed in a neat console panel between driver and passenger. Warning lights for ignition and oil pressure are also on the console, along with the various switches. The horn button is on the instrument panel and, on the right-hand-drive model, is within finger reach of the wood-rimmed alloy spoked steering wheel. This wheel is adjustable and can be moved to suit any driving style, even for drivers well over 6 feet tall.

So much for the outside. What's new under the bonnet is the Ford 105-E engine. At the present moment this is sold stock with a single carburetor producing 39 bhp at 5000 rpm, but a version with twin carburetors, high lift cams, and modified exhaust and inlet manifolds will be available shortly as an optional extra.

Ford components have also been used in the transmission, the 4-wheel independent suspension and in various

other places about the car. The power is transmitted through a Ford 105-E clutch and gearbox and goes to the rear wheels via a Ford differential modified to provide independent suspension. The final drive ratio is 4.125:1. Steering is by means of a Triumph Herald rack and pinion box which gives a turning circle of 29 ft.

The frame is made of 20 gauge steel, with 10 gauge at the stress points. The main side members and other members are made up from two U sections spot-welded together. For true sporting types, the body can be lifted off and the chassis run bare.

An unusual feature of the Bandit is the gasoline filler opening, which has a sort of plated drip tray around it with a drain hole. With a realistic distrust of fuel gauges, Mr. Panter says a dip stick can be used to check fuel level.

The trunk, which is actually a shade larger than that of the Triumph TR, has the spare wheel stowed under a platform on the floor. There is also a fair-sized carpeted space behind the seats, with large door pockets and a lockable compartment built into the center arm rest (which, however, can't be opened with bottom or top gear engaged).

The available options include a heater and de-mister, external luggage carrier, twin horns, over-all tonneau cover, safety harness, a larger capacity fuel tank, "Track Grip" tires and, in the U.S., a roll bar. A detachable hardtop will soon be made available and may be the fast-back type. Wire wheels may come later, but at present the car gets along on its 13-in. pressed steel discs.

Beginning our short performance run, the Bandit got away to a very promising start, but it soon became obvious that there was a flat spot somewhere. The performance higher up was disappointing, to say the least. I was told the mechanics had been so busy getting the suspension right they hadn't had time to work on the engine.

One thing is certain, though; they definitely have got the suspension right. Along the straights the ride is firm but not uncomfortable, just like a dozen other cars, but on the corners it comes into its own. The Bandit simply does not roll and there is no tire squeal at all. The braking is entirely adequate, too, with 8-in. discs on the front and 8-in. drums at the rear. It is obvious that the car will motor far faster than the stock Ford will let it.

In England the Bandit will cost about $2250 in its standard form, including the stiff purchase tax. By comparison, the Sprite price is about $1780 in Britain. The new Berkeley should be available in the U.S. around March.   —*Eric Wiseman and R. L. Simpson*

Berkeley Threewheeler

INCREASED REAR SEAT accommodation is the principal modification of the new deluxe version of the Berkeley Three-Wheeler. Introduced in September 1959 by Berkeley Cars Limited, Biggleswade, more than 1700 of these spirited little cars have been sold.

In addition to the enlarged rear seat, the windshield has been redesigned to give better visibility, and a larger hood has been provided. A heavy-duty front suspension has been incorporated, and a reinforced rear suspension incorporates a larger spring shock absorber unit and enables a lower sitting position to be provided. The body is constructed of molded glass fiber. Wheel discs are included as standard equipment.

The little three-wheeler is powered by an Excelsior 328cc twin-cylinder engine and the drive is to the front wheels. Top speed is said to be 55 to 60 miles per hour and the manufacturer claims fuel consumption of 60 miles per gallon. Price of the deluxe model is about $1275, while the standard model runs at $1197.

Berkeley Cars recently introduced its newly designed, deluxe three-wheel car. Increased space in the rear seat tops the main changes from previous models. Powered by an Excelsior 328 cc twin cylinder engine, and with front-wheel drive, fuel consumption of 60 miles per gallon is claimed.

Short and Sharp

The production of Berkeley cars lasted only five years. **Nigel Halliday** traces the history of this short-lived but interesting marque.

DURING the late 1950s small and miniature cars, often powered by motorcycle engines, were built by several companies. The aim was to produce cheap, economical motoring in the wake of the Suez crisis, and later for the lower end of the market. Among the manufacturers were Bond, Reliant, Goggomobil, Messerschmitt, Frisky, Nobel, Peel, Gordon, Unicar and Berkeley — names now mostly forgotten.

The Berkeleys were particularly interesting as they had style, a sporting character, lively performance and offered the joys of drophead coupe motoring. They were built in Biggleswade, Bedfordshire, by Berkeley Coachwork Limited under the chairmanship of Mr Charles Panter who, during the war, had been managing a relocated furniture manufacturing company from Edmonton in north London. This company was located on a Bedfordshire airfield (Old Warden) and repaired wooden-built aeroplanes as part of the war effort. After the war, Panter found he had surplus labour and many new techniques at his fingertips, so he started making caravans. Over the next three years, during which the name

Short and Sharp

factory were changed, Berkeley Coachwork produced a large number of highly regarded caravans. They also pioneered many new techniques, especially glassfibre and lightweight sandwich construction. The fortunes of the company were very good until 1955 when a fall in demand led to Charles Panter looking for new products. At that time car sales were booming and he reasoned that there was a market niche for a small economical sports car.

At about the same time, Laurie Bond was looking for a manufacturer to produce a lightweight sports car he had designed. Hearing of Charles Panter's success with glass-reinforced plastics, the two met and decided to collaborate. Laurie Bond styled his basic design of an alloy and glassfibre-constructed lightweight car powered by a motorcycle two-stroke engine into a prototype suitable for production by Panter. The next step — production engineering and testing — was rather hurried so that Berkeley's could be at the 1956 Motor Show. The highly publicised launch of the car included BBC and Newsreel cameras filming Stirling Moss driving at Goodwood.

The first model was called the Berkeley Sports, an open two-seater. It was formed from three basic body sections — the punt-shaped chassis of glassfibre and aluminium box sections, sills and bulkheads; the front section and bonnet, formed again of glassfibre and aluminium bulkheads; and the rear section which was a unitary glassfibre moulding. Separate mouldings were used for the bonnet, doors and rear seat cover.

Power came from an Anzani 322cc two-stroke twin driving a primary chain and Albion multi-plate clutch to a three-speed motorcycle gearbox. A single driving chain then passed back to a small spur-wheel differential designed and built by Berkeley themselves. Final drive was transmitted to the front wheels by Hardy Spicer splined driveshafts and universal joints. This whole power unit was situated ahead of the front wheels giving the 'sports' a relatively long, sleek bonnet.

Suspension was independent with unequal length wishbones at the front and swing axles at the rear located by large wishbones. Armstrong or Girling motorbike springs with integral telescopic dampers completed the arrangement. Steering was by nut and worm steering box as used on Fords at the time, with small track rods to the cast hubs.

Braking, always very efficient in Berkeleys, was by a Girling hydraulic system of twin cylinders on the front wheels and single compensating one at the rear. The handbrake was cable and rod-operated from an umbrella handle mounted beneath the dashboard, although on other models this was later changed to a floor mounting. The brakes operated against cast hubs which were unusual in having a five-stud fixing for the pressed steel wheels, carrying 5.20-12in Michelin tyres. A Siba Dynastart, mounted on the flywheel, silently started the engine and then took over as a Dynamo.

Externally, the Sports could be said to have a stubby 'E-type' front and an Austin Healey Sprite rear, but the designer Laurie Bond had obviously beaten these models by several years. The inside was basic and the space requirements kept to a minimum. The low lines of the car meant that the occupants virtually sat on the floor on a strap-webbed squab seat. The soft-top canvas hood was often supported by human skulls rather than the metal frame hoops!

Performance was impressive considering the small 322cc engine. Maximum speed was claimed to be 70mph but 60mph was generally about the maximum ever obtained in road tests. Acceleration from 0 to 50mph was around 30sec but seemed a lot quicker due to the closeness of the road. Economy was even better — 50-60mpg. After six months and an alleged production of 100 units per week (in retrospect, it was more like 100 Anzani units in total) the power unit was changed to an Excelsior Twin Talisman two-stroke of 328cc and the gearchange moved from the steering column to a floor mounted quadrant.

At the 1957 Motor Show the Sports was shown with various improvements in body detail and was joined by the Sports Deluxe which was available in fixedhead coupe and drophead version. The Deluxe had various refinements and extras such as polished wheel trims, wheel spinners and tachometer, but the major change was to fit twin Amal carburettors. Berkeley also offered an optional three-cylinder 492cc version of the Excelsior engine, specifically developed by Excelsior for Berkeley. It produced 30bhp at 5500rpm as opposed to the 18bhp of the twin.

The fixed-head coupe with the three-cylinder was in fact the centrepiece of the Berkeley stand at the Motor Show, but no further examples of this particular coupe model have been seen or heard of since.

Many Berkeleys were exported, especially to the USA; the cars were designed from the start for left or right-hand drive. Several very large export orders were also mentioned by the local press at the time, but it seems unlikely that Berkeleys reached the production figures necessary to fulfil these large orders.

It was also apparent at about this time that several defects were showing in the basic design. The chassis section lacked rigidity, causing flexing, which often meant the doors flew open on bumpy corners. The front damper/spring units, mounted on to the glassfibre and alloy bulkheads, eventually punched their way through. There was also a production run of bad body mouldings supposedly caused by faulty resins. Many mouldings had to be thrown away.

Excelsior produced a 30bhp version of their three-cylinder engine for Berkeley to offer as an option in the sports model.

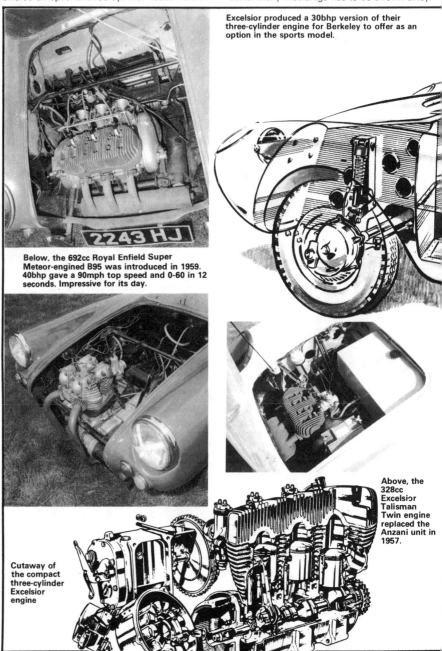

Below, the 692cc Royal Enfield Super Meteor-engined B95 was introduced in 1959. 40bhp gave a 90mph top speed and 0-60 in 12 seconds. Impressive for its day.

Above, the 328cc Excelsior Talisman Twin engine replaced the Anzani unit in 1957.

Cutaway of the compact three-cylinder Excelsior engine

There was in fact a court case over this matter which lasted three years between the resin manufacturers and Berkeley. The chassis problem was never really solved although the later steel chassis helped. The front damper units were also reinforced with vertical steel channels introduced adjacent to the bulkhead, and a transverse member was mounted across the engine bay.

The engine was relatively long lived although a rebuild needed great care as the fabricated crankshaft had to be very carefully lined up to avoid distortion; the 492 was particularly prone to this problem because of its extended crankshaft. These various deficiencies meant heavy warranty claims and a deteriorating relationship between dealers, buyers and factory.

Four family seats
At the 1958 Motor Show, Berkeley introduced the Foursome, which was an enlarged version of the ordinary Sports Twosome but powered by the 492cc three-cylinder engine. The basic design was similar to the two-seater except it was 8in longer and 4in wider; it was fitted with a rear bench and single front bucket seats, the spare wheel being moved to a rear mounting with a cover on the back of the car. The models came with side screens and hood or an optional hardtop. An interesting feature, which unfortunately was not used again on other models, was that the rear suspension subframe and A brackets were mounted below the punt chassis in a recessed pocket. This had the effect of lowering the suspension and making the roadholding even better. Unfortunately the Fourcome was rather cramped and suffered from severe body flexing, although the front and rear suspension points were improved. Production of the Foursome ceased after only 22 cars, so it's the rarest of all the Berkeleys.

Since their introduction owners and press had criticised the lack of power, so in March 1959 after a spell of testing and development with Royal Enfield, Berkeley launched the 792cc Royal Enfield Super Meteor-engined B95. The car was basically similar to the Sports except the front had a higher bonnet line with a square nose and slatted air intake. The wings also ended in ordinary Lucas headlamps as opposed to the earlier flared-in Wipac units. The four-stroke air-cooled twin, mounted at the front of the car on a small frame between the side members and bulkheads, had a conventional starter motor and dynamo. The rest of the car was unaltered except for small details. A more powerful variant, called the B105, had a higher compression ratio version of the 792cc Meteor engine giving 50bhp at 6250rpm against the 40bhp at 5500rpm of the B95. These models had a top speed of over 90mph and a 0-60mph acceleration of about 12 seconds, making them very respectable performers.

Both the four-strokes sold moderately well, a good proportion being exported. The earlier sports model was then dropped in favour of another new model, the T60, launched in August 1959. This three-wheel T60 became the most common Berkeley, enjoying more success than any other model because it attracted ex-motor cyclists looking for low running costs. It also had better roadholding, performance and a more sporting appearance than other three wheelers.

The mechanical design and general features of

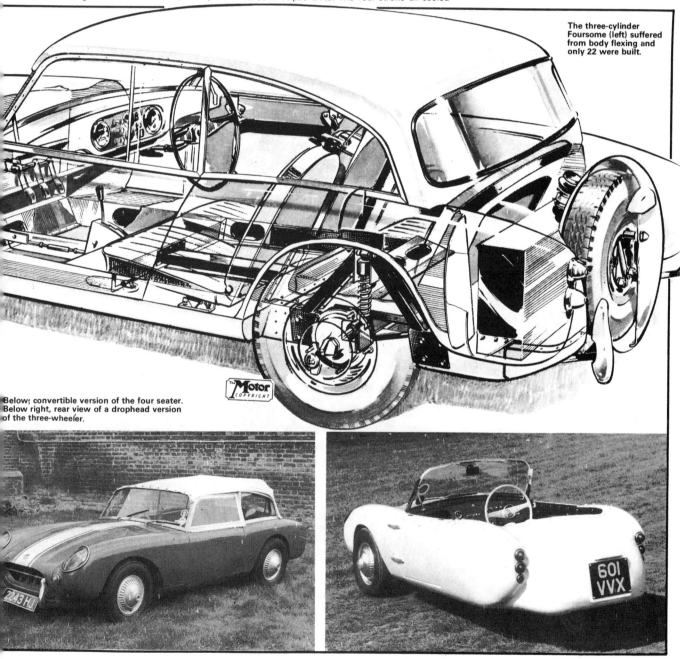

The three-cylinder Foursome (left) suffered from body flexing and only 22 were built.

Below; convertible version of the four seater. Below right, rear view of a drophead version of the three-wheeler.

Short and Sharp

the new car were the same as the standard 'Sports' model with the exception of the rear body mouldings which accommodated the single rear wheel which was mounted centrally on a single arm, swinging from a metal crossmember moulded in the glass fibre chassis at the base of the rear seat. The arm also had a telescopic spring/damper unit which was later uprated to overcome grounding. The remainder of the equipment followed the Sports model with a few minor detail changes. The main body difference was the bulbous rear end (to accommodate the central rear wheel), and the doors were now fitted with internal rather than external hinges and vertical rather than sloping door posts. The T60 stiffening alloy chassis members were changed to steel in 1960, giving the model a rust problem in later life, although restoration is straightforward as new steel sections are easy to fabricate.

In July 1960, Berkeley announced an improved four-seater model, the T60/4. This was essentially a T60 but the parcel shelf was lowered and moved back, giving a slight bump-shape to the rear seat due to the wheel arch intrusion. The model also featured some former deluxe-model items such as a fuel gauge, wheel trims and mock spinners.

The suspension of the T60/4 was stiffened and the windscreen mounted in glass fibre rather than chromed brass frame. The general air of the car is one of a marketing/sales exercise in the face of the 'company problems', but without any real development work for a full four-seater car behind it. Berkeley had already employed these tactics a few months before when they launched two variants on the B95 model called the Q95 and the QB95 but these were only ever seen at the 1959 Motor Show and were in fact the existing B95 model widened by 4 inches and lengthened by 8 inches and fitted with alternative front seats. The QB95 was a full two-seater with adjustable front bucket seats and a parcel shelf area behind, whereas the Q95 had a front bench seat and an occasional rear bench seat.

Enter the Bandit

At the 1960 Motor Show, Berkeley re-introduced the Sports model and called it the B95. They also showed a B95 and a prototype of their new model, the Bandit. The latter was commissioned by Berkeley in early 1960 in an attempt to enter the more traditional sports car market. It was designed by John Tojeiro and two development prototypes were built. The Bandit was in an up-to-date style with some interesting engineering, and it diverged from the usual Berkeley practice in that it had an aluminium and steel chassis with a separate glass fibre body, both constructed more substantially than in previous models. The power unit and drive chain were taken from the Ford 105E Anglia although there was provision for larger engines. Drive was to the rear wheels but Berkeley retained a swing axle layout with combined coil spring and damper units acting on the hub. To accommodate this layout, the Anglia differential was modified by removing the axle tubes and replacing the half-shafts with two universal joints · and sliding splines. Front suspension was by MacPherson strut. Disc brakes were fitted at the front and modified Anglia drum brakes at the rear. The interior was well finished with a padded leather dashboard and console, adjustable bucket seats, door map pockets.

Several road tests of the prototypes gave very good accounts of its performance and roadholding but the company itself was failing and the model never entered production. The actual demise of Berkeley Coachwork Limited came on the 9th February 1961 when the company was declared bankrupt and formally wound up. The Chairman of the creditors remarked that a disproportionate amount of money had been spent on research and development from which there was no profit. He further added that there was a very substantial loss from July 1959 onwards and he thought it was probably due to overproduction, bearing in mind the general economic conditions of the time. He also suggested that there had been a lack of proper financial control and foresight before starting new projects, such as the Bandit, with the result that the company had overtraded on its capital.

At the time of the Bankruptcy reports in January 1961, it was stated that 2500 cars and 1700 T60 tricycles had been made. Allowing for export of the four-wheelers, quite a large proportion of cars have survived in the UK; at least 200 are known to the Berkeley Enthusiasts Club.

Sporting achievements

An interesting side of Berkeley history was their involvement in motor sport. From 1956, Berkeley set out on a racing programme either with a Factory team or by sponsoring other competitors. The earliest report of a competition Berkeley was at the Blackpool & Fylde Motor Club meeting of the 2nd November 1956 when Tony Marsh put up an impressive performance in the 1300cc class. This promising start spurred the works to set up a competition department. The Berkeley team comprised Sports models either in 328cc or later 492cc form driving in the GT category of races amongst other sports cars. The most successful driver was J Goddard-Watts who ended the 1958 season second in the Autosport championship class award for cars up to 1000cc in front of third-placed R A Jamieson, another Berkeley driver.

The following year saw Berkeley competitors changing to the 692cc-engined cars with further successes, particularly in driving tests in which Ian Mantle (a Berkeley dealer in Bedfordshire) seemed to excel. 1959 was also a year of international Berkeley recognition for Italian Count Lurani assembled a team with drivers, Cammarata and Bandini, to compete in the 500cc GT class. The cars used were modified 492cc sports models and they achieved outright success in the 500cc Monza 12-hour race in April 1959 with an average speed of 76mph, and again at the Monza Grand Prix in September when a 492cc hardtop sports model driven by Largarialli beat racing Fiats by four laps. Similar outright wins were also recorded during the year at Verona.

At home another Berkeley driver, Wing Commander George Catt, was also achieving success and admiration for his courage and driving skills with a B105 in local and national and club races. Unfortunately he had a bad accident in the car whilst driving at Snetterton and died as a result of his injuries.

Berkeleys were also taken rallying. One report of the 1958 Thames Estuary Auto Club, 'Cat's Eye Rally' notes that a Berkeley which had gone into a ditch was literally lifted back on to the road! There were also several Berkeley entries in the 1958 Tulip Rally and the 1959 Monte Carlo Rally, but unfortunately, the cars were either disqualified or withdrawn due to mechanical problems.

The various Berkeleys are now firmly established with classic enthusiasts as they are interesting, economical and fun to drive. They are also especially suitable for restoration as their designed construction demands few special tools or skills. Most models can be purchased very reasonably unrestored, although restored examples, especially the four-wheeler B95 and B105 can fetch quite large sums.

Motorcycle restoration specialists can help with the engines and transmission spares, although Excelsior parts are now nearly exhausted. Most ancillaries on the car such as brakes, lights and instruments are standard parts from Girling, AC, Lucas and Wipac. Berkeley owners also have the help of the Berkeley Enthusiast Club (Secretary — D J Price, 17 Cherry Tree Avenue, London Colney, St Albans, Herts). This is an enthusiastic club with a membership of around 120, and it provides a magazine and newsletter. Although the club doesn't yet itself deal with spares, Berkeley Developments, a specialist firm, can supply many parts and some information; they can be found at 6 Wollaton Road, Chaddesden, Derby.

Four-wheeler interior showing its spartan nature and the limited equipment

The cockpit of the three-wheeler is similarly spartan but even more cramped.

Side view of the T60 three-wheeler. Note the tail-up attitude and the bulbous rear wheel housing.

Enfield-engined Berkeleys can be recognised by the high-profile front.

Fifties Superbomb!

How Berkeley fought for a pedigree — by Bernie Pearson, of the Berkeley Enthusiasts Club

WHEN, in the winter of 1955, Charles Panter's caravan company, Berkeley Coachworks, shivered in the chill wind of its annual production low-season, thoughts once more turned to finding an alternative product to keep his skilled labour force busy. The arrival at the Berkshire factory of Laurie Bond, designer of the quirky but commercially successful Minicar, must have seemed a Godsend when he unfurled his artists impression of a tiny four-wheeled micro sportscar. T Panter's company, already well respected for their pioneering work in the new technology of glass reinforced polyester resins, the all-fibreglass monocoque construction offered a means of employing all their skills and experience in a venture less affected by the seasonal demands of caravaning. Bond's new baby was unlike anything then available, though typically it employed motorcycle-type engine and

transmission. Bond had approached several likely prospects in his search for someone to manufacture his brainchild, among them Oppermans of Borehamwood, but on hearing of Berkeley's successes in the first really large-scale commercial use of fibreglass he made an appointment with Charles Panter, a man renowned for his progressive and innovative thinking. In the black ceilinged office in Hitchin Street, Biggleswade, Panter negotiated a deal; that done and with characteristic drive, he put his team into top gear. It was already early Spring and he wanted the new car to be at the Earls Court Motor Show in October. The design of the car aided rapid progress. The whole body — chassis monocoque was constructed from only three major

mouldings — a long flat undertray which incorporated light aluminium box-section sills, a nose section reinforced by aluminium bulkheads, and a tail which included a small moulded "dickey-seat". In spite of a relatively thin lay-up each moulding made maximum use of the rigidity gained from the use of multiple curvature and, when rivetted together, the three sections formed a remarkably stiff and extremely light shell.

The rest of the car was a carefully blended mixture of established sportscar design and eccentric inventionism. Bond's experience of racing car design, in itself a study in non-conformity, had been drawn from several years of campaigning an own-design front wheel drive Norton-powered hill climber. The Berkeley therefore utilised unequal length parallel wishbones at the front and swing axles at the rear and a shape which, even to the cynical, pays a pretty compliment to the AC Ace amongst others. It was in the choice of motive

The Bandit which used Ford Anglia running gear and with Ford backing could have mounted a major challenge to the profitable Sprites and Midgets — this one-off prototype Berkeley could have saved the company but Ford gave the idea the thumbs down.

Fifties Superbomb!

power, though, that the Berkeley Sports raised most eyebrows.

In a world just recovering from the exhaustion of war and the privations and shortages that accompanied it, the all-pervading hope was of a new deal and a better life for all. Personal transport was one expression of the new freedom and a whole gamut of low-cost economical answers to the demand erupted onto the road in the form of what rapidly became known as bubble-cars. Mostly motorcycle engined — and with comfort and controls that owed

The T.60 three-wheeler, Berkeley's most successful model. Like Austin Seven Sports, 20 years before, it provided cheap and sporting fun.

A prototype 500cc Coupe — none survive. Note the AC rear wing and Healey-styled hard-top — quite a pleasing design.

with supply and reliability of the Anzani engine had resulted in a switch to the slightly more powerful but otherwise similar 328cc Excelsior two-stroke twin. With 18bhp available, a 20% increase over the Anzani, the production model achieved a 0-50 time of 10 seconds (one up) and a figure of 60 miles per rationed gallon.

A carefully orchestrated press release guaranteed nationwide coverage of the launch, and the young racing superstar Stirling Moss gave the car his guarded blessing in a Goodwood track test televised in BBC's *Sportsview*. His suggestion that the unconventional front wheel drive might cause the inexperienced some problems would cause a wry smile in today's almost

little to the science of ergonomics — they were essentially a simple means of moving from A to B. And none too reliable.

What Panter and Bond wanted to achieve was "Something good enough to win World 750cc races ... but cheap, safe, easily repairable, reliable and pretty", admirable ambitions which were almost fully realised. Had not these same ambitions been deemed worthy of serious consideration in various Austin Seven sporting cars of 20 years before?

Their choice of the 322cc Anzani two-stroke twin was perhaps not as odd as might be thought in the light of today's thinking, nor was the chain drive. In fact, when one considers that the Berkeley employed a transverse engine, front wheel drive and dimensions which make a Mini look like a limousine, all some two years before the introduction of the British Leyland blockbuster, it can be appreciated why the Berkeley was received in a blaze of publicity.

Performance with the two-stroke, assisted by its incredibly low all up weight of just 6½cwt, was more than a match for its costly competitors and earned for the car the title of the "Poor Man's Safe Sportscar", a headline which the *Daily Mail* followed up with "... and it's *British!*" But it was in its braking and roadholding that the Berkeley really made the Press sit up and take notice. 7" Girling brakes all round stopping less than seven

Smiles of pride — the small team around the first Berkeley to be made.

hundredweight inspired John Bolster in *Autosport* to compare it with a Formula Junior, and handling "... which challenged one's courage and discretion" set the car firmly in the middle of an identity crisis, which was to result in ever bigger-engined versions.

From the very start the car lacked the power to match its looks. By the time production was under way, problems

totally F.W.D. world. But he was right in his prediction that it would appeal to those who were looking for a beginning in motor sport. Before long Berkeleys began to appear on the circuits of Britain in David and Goliath dices with machinery of considerably greater capacity.

In rallies, too, the tiny two-strokes made a name for themselves and they

One-marque racing at a very basic Brands Hatch -- Berkeleys captured imaginations.

were almost unbeatable in autotests. Their combination of superb brakes, leech-like roadholding and inately chuckable handling more than compensated for what they lacked in cubic centimetres. Even at the press launch, announcements were being made of a larger-engined version of the Sports. Work had already begun on adapting a BSA 500cc four-stroke twin for use in the car when an engineer from the Birmingham-based Excelsior motorcycle works arrived with two prototypes of a new engine in the boot

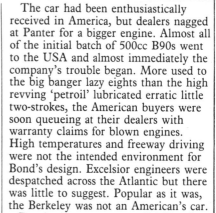

Big 692cc Royal Enfield called for a higher nose line.

Square-nose pushed up Prescott — performance was now very exciting indeed.

of his Jaguar. Because the crankcases on the 328cc twin Excelsior were divided on the cylinder centre-line, it had proved possible to "insert" another cylinder between those of the twin. The resultant 3-cylinder engine produced a turbine smooth 30bhp on a slightly lower compression ratio and breathing through three Amal monobloc carburettors. The main appeal of the solution to Charles Panter was that the new engine was almost a straight swap for the twin. In fact, as soon as supplies began to arrive, Berkeley fitters began removing twins to fit triples.

The car had been enthusiastically received in America, but dealers nagged at Panter for a bigger engine. Almost all of the initial batch of 500cc B90s went to the USA and almost immediately the company's trouble began. More used to the big banger lazy eights than the high revving 'petroil' lubricated erratic little two-strokes, the American buyers were soon queueing at their dealers with warranty claims for blown engines. High temperatures and freeway driving were not the intended environment for Bond's design. Excelsior engineers were despatched across the Atlantic but there was little to suggest. Popular as it was, the Berkeley was not an American's car.

Despite its apparent unreliability the Excelsior unit in 500cc triple form proved that, given sufficient attention, it was a world beater. Count "Johnny" Lurani, a well-known and respected motor racing entrant and driver, bought three B90s in left-hand drive form and entered them in various races in Europe in the 750cc G.T. category for which they were fitted with an extremely attractive aluminium hardtop of his own design. At Verona, the 12-hour race at

Stretched four-seater — only 19 were produced.

Fifties Superbomb!

Monza and in the 1958 Mille Miglia the Berkeleys shocked the establishment by beating the works Fiats and Stanguellinis. Several times they even won their class in the European Hill Climb Championship.

Pat Moss entered a "little Liège" rally, an event for small cars only, across Europe. She drove a cream Berkeley, TBM 11, and revelled in its excellent handling. In her book, *The Story So Far*, Pat describes taking mountain hairpins flat out. The team of three had oil/petrol mixture problems, and all three retired with seized-up engines.

But still the search for more power went on though choice of suitable power units became more and more limited. The design of the car and its minimal dimensions precluded all but motorcycle units and even then four-stroke twins were too tall for the sleek wind-cheating bonnet line.

Styling remained unchanged, apart that is from a prototype fixed head coupe which didn't see production and a stretched family "foursome" version of which only 19 left the line. However, when the Royal Enfield 692cc twin was finally chosen as the new motive force a radical change was brought about in the shape of the nose section. A four-stroke valve gear made the engine almost twice as tall as the two-stroke and a lump that size needed plenty of air for its cooling. 1959 therefore saw the introduction of the very different looking B95. A large

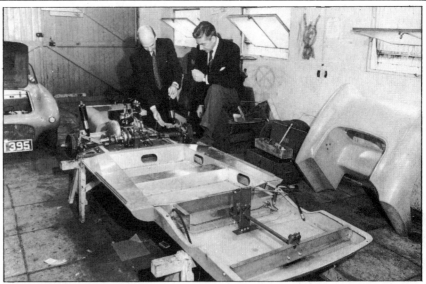

Laurie Bond and Charles Panter cast a critical eye during construction.

Body being hand-made.

Works prototype at Goodwood, 1957.

vertical rectangular opening supplied the coolant and a higher bonnet line covered the relatively massive engine unit. Exposed headlights replaced the fairings of the earlier models and gave the new car a brutish, some say ugly, appearance. But it did go!

With 40bhp available to push 7cwt, performance was breathtaking. To floor the right foot was to unleash a great thundering crashing surge of acceleration which, when 5" from the tarmac, paled the face and whitened the knuckles of all but the brave or foolhardy. On the circuits it was an

instant winner without the help of the handicappers. The newly introduced Austin Healey Sprite could keep up only in the hands of the most adept of drivers and Jon Goddard-Watts, by then the official Berkeley Works entrant, enjoyed many a dice on the club circuits to the amusement of the applauding spectators.

Commercially the company were losing ground. The Sprite with its conventional water-cooled four-stroke four and normal layout carried more appeal to the weekend sportscar fan, and the Mini had now become the classless second car or cheap family transport. Even with hindsight it is difficult to understand why the factory missed out on their greatest market area. With bubble and other microcars continuing to sell well to the ex-motorcyclist market and with Britain's tax laws favouring the three-wheeler, it might perhaps appear that the Biggleswade factory were a little tardy in announcing their biggest-selling model — the T60. Identical to the successful B65 models from the seats forward and with the familiar 328cc Excelsior engine, the new trike was met with great interest by the motorcycle press. It offered handling almost as astonishing as the four-wheeler, the same superb brakes and an engine and

transmission with which the motorcycle fraternity would feel quite at home. In the year of its announcement almost 2,000 T60s were built, a figure which closely matches the total production figure of all models of four-wheelers over the previous three years.

A clue to the reasoning may be found in the project which so nearly saved the company. Faced with opposition from the Sprite, Panter, who still thought of Berkeleys as a sportscar manufacturer rather than a microcar factory, sought a solution in the shape of a much more conventional car. The Bandit, as the new model was christened, was to utilise the recently introduced Ford Anglia 105E mechanicals as a basis for a totally new concept. Front engine rear wheel drive replaced the FWD of previous Berkeleys, a steel chassis took the place of the fibreglass monocoque and the standard of trim was far removed from the spartan austerity of the early cars. Two prototypes were produced with John Tojeiro engaged as consultant in suspension design.

On their appearance at the Earls Court Show in 1960 there was a great deal of interest shown, not only from the public but also from the motor industry establishment. Ford's product development team, already engaged in a study of the sportscar market, were most interested in what was effectively the Anglia Sports. Had Ford not shelved the idea or Berkeley's bankers not got cold feet, had the caravan trade been in a boom period or the factory not over-produced, then the story might well have been of triumph and success. In fact, a series of minor crises, none of which individually would have worried the dynamic fighter that was Panter, conspired to bring a once successful business to its knees.

On December 13th, 1960, Charles Panter faced his workforce in the staff canteen with the news that the company was in the hands of the Receiver. The days of the Fifties Superbomb were over.

BERKELEY T60

BERKELEY T60	Styling	Handling	Perform'ce	Practicality	Comfort	Drivability	Total%
SJ	8	8	7	5	7	7	70
BG	9	10	9	9	9	10	93
RB	9	8	7	6	7	9	77
DG	9	10	10	8	7	9	88
MT	9	9	10	8	8	9	88

Our testers' results

Steve Jefferys: "The Berkeley looks stylish and has a great driving position, even for someone over six feet tall. Space inside is adequate and the controls, including brakes and gearbox, are very good. Performance is very impressive, handling responsive and cornering excellent: this is a real driver's car."

Bob Goodwin: "Styling is superb – it's probably the best-looking microcar. On twisty roads, hold your nerve, keep off the brakes, and get a terrific thrill. This could be a great bird-puller, similar to an E-type! It's more roomy than it appears, controls are basic but adequate and the steering lacks self-centring, but it does all a sports car should. The exhaust may be anti-social but it gives lots of pleasure!"

Ralph Beardsmore: "This is what a sports car should look like, and it's comfortable with plenty of leg room once you're in, but I found the steering wheel too close to my chest. The gears are easy to find but you do need to double-declutch down the gate. Cornering is excel-lent, the car doesn't wander but the driveshafts judder when pulling away on lock. Fun to drive."

David Green: "A sporty-looking car that seems to fit around you like a glove once you're inside. I found it a bit wayward on the steering and kept hitting the indicator switch with my knee. The gearchange is a fine art but the engine lives on revs and the car is fun to drive; it can be pushed to the limits. It corners on rails and is a real driver's car: a bit more refined than my Scootacar!"

Malcolm Thomas: "The Berkeley interior is basic in the Fifties sports car style and space is a bit restricted. Controls are all in the right position though it's not always easy to find a gear in a hurry. Performance is very lively from just 328cc with a good ride, no roll and positive steering (though it doesn't self-centre). It's a good sports car – great fun – I wish I hadn't sold mine!"

Malcolm McKay: "As a fellow Berkeley owner I should abstain, except to say Mike's T60 went better than mine ever has and on the twisty, narrow country roads we used it really would give many bigger sports cars a run for their money. Well-maintained Berkeleys are enormous fun and deserve a better reputation than they have."

Transverse front engine and front-wheel drive appeared on the Berkeley before the Mini! Spare wheel should fit under the dashboard

1960 Berkeley T60

Price new:	£399 (1960)
Price now:	£2,000
Engine:	Excelsior 328cc twin (two-stroke)
Layout:	Transverse front engine, front-wheel drive
Gearbox:	Albion 4-speed + reverse
Power:	18bhp at 5,000rpm
Top speed:	60mph
Fuel consumption:	59mpg
Kerb weight:	763lb
Parts availability:	70%

Mike Musselwhite, a 57-year-old cycle mechanic, has owned an early four-wheeler Berkeley for 10 years and the T60 for four. A keen member of the Berkeley Enthusiasts Club, he recalls: "When I bought the T60 it was in boxes, totally stripped: only the metal parts of the structure had been restored. I finished the restoration four weeks ago, using an engine that had been under a bench for 15 years. I've done 56 miles since putting it on the road so this test will more than double that!"

Baby Berkeley

B aby boomer: the term instantly evokes images of the generation born in the immediate post war period as young couples got back together again after years of separation or postponed courting because of the war.

The baby boomers grew up in the 1950s and 1960s, a population bulge which successively placed almost insupportable demands on the Plunket Society, the education system, the housing market and the Plunket Society again as they started having their own children. They will, we are told, cripple the country's economy in another 20-30 years with their demands on the superannuation scheme.

But the baby boomer we are discussing here, while it was a product of the same post war years, does not place many

Bill Hobbs looks at a very small British sports car from the 1950s…

demands on anything - except perhaps the nerves of the driver in heavy traffic.

Certainly its dimensions of 10'6" (3200mm) overall length, 4'2" (1270mm) wide and 2'6" (762mm) high show it does not place great demands on road or garage space. With a twin cylinder motor-cycle engine to power it the demands it puts on the world's stock of fossil fuels cannot be too great either.

It is unquestionably a baby among baby cars.

It is also quite a boomer, because this is

the Berkeley model B95, a designation which remarkably stands for a top speed of 95 mph (145km/h). There was even a version with a more highly tuned version of the same engine designated B105.

However, it must be conceded that not all Berkeleys were such boomers in their performance, most of them being far more docile babies.

The Berkeley sports car came about through an association between Laurie Bond of mini car fame and Charles Panter of Berkeley Caravans, while searching for something his factory could manufacture during the off season.

One of the strengths of Berkeley Caravans was that in the early 1950s the company was one of the leaders in the use of GRP, otherwise known as glass

Jack Bier's Royal Enfield-engined Berkeley sports car in Nelson.

reinforced plastic or fibreglass. This was the material Laurie Bond wanted to use in the construction of a small sports car he had designed.

Bond sold the manufacturing rights to Charles Panter and the Berkeley sports car was born.

It first appeared in 1956 powered by a 322cc Anzani two stroke engine with an output of 15bhp. This was quickly replaced by the 328cc Excelsior Talisman twin engine with the better output of 18bhp.

The car looked good but its top speed of something around 65mph (105km/h) was modest even by the standards of mid 1950s small cars so the company started looking at more powerful engine units. About this time Excelsior came up with a three cylinder version of the Talisman and its 500cc and 30bhp output gave the Berkeley the sort of performance that went with its looks.

In this form the little Berkeley started to notch up a number of wins in small capacity racing, particularly in Italy where Count Johnny Lurani ran a team of three cars in events such as the Monza 12 hours. Stirling Moss was also enticed to drive the car in the odd event.

However, overall the three cylinder Excelsior was not a success in commercial terms because of unreliability and warranty problems. Another try with a more powerful engine saw the adoption of the 700cc Royal Enfield parallel twin engine.

This was available as the 40bhp Royal Enfield Super Meteor, as used in the B95, or as the even more powerful Constellation with 50bhp on tap. The latter version is used in the B105.

About 40 Berkeley sports cars were exported to New Zealand in the mid to late 1950s out of the 2000 or so four wheel cars built. There was also a three wheeled version built in even bigger numbers for the British domestic market. It was known as the T (for tricycles) 60 model.

The vast majority of the four wheel cars and all the three wheelers were fitted with the twin cylinder version of the Excelsior, as were all the cars imported to New Zealand.

One exception is the B95 model imported a couple of years ago by Jack Bier of Nelson and recently put back on the road after extensive restoration.

Jack is not an enthusiast for small 1950s British sports cars as such but he is a long time enthusiast for Royal Enfield motorcycles. When the opportunity arose through an acquaintance in England to buy a Royal Enfield engined car the temptation proved irresistible.

The car arrived in May 1988 showing 30,000 miles on the clock but a badly worn engine which suggested they had been rather hard miles on the whole. Disappointingly the car had also suffered some damage in transit which made the

job of restoration a little harder than anticipated.

On the credit side the car, although a little battered, was complete in every detail, even down to the Berkeley hub caps with their "B" emblem and dummy wing nuts.

Restoring the engine posed no great problems as it is virtually identical to the Royal Enfield motorcycle engine which Jack knows so well. The only differences he noted were a longer driveshaft in the Berkeley to accommodate a pulley for the car's 12 volt generator and a heavier flywheel for better idling.

Even the exhaust pipes back to the muffler were straight off a motorcycle,

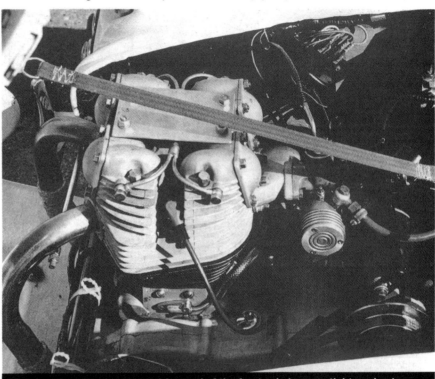

Motorcycle engine is mounted forward of the front axle in some tight packaging.

though extended somewhat at the rear.

The drive is also common to Royal Enfield motorcycles in many respects, at least in the primary stages. The engine is located well to the front and drives by chain to a four plate Albion clutch and Albion gearbox.

There is a further chain drive then to the differential and two halfshafts which take the power to the front wheels. It is all straightforward but a little cramped for space, as a consequence of which Jack says it would help to have fingers like octopus tentacles to work on the car.

With all the mechanical parts ahead of the axle there is ample leg room in the cockpit despite the miniscule size of the car. There is even enough room for some storage in the footwell on the passenger's side, which is probably as well given the

lack of storage space elsewhere.

There are cavities in the doors for small items and a small boot behind the seats, the only part of the car which can be locked up. Even at best there is only space there for a couple of smallish soft bags and not even that when the hood and side screens are stowed.

Jack has a small luggage rack on his car to provide extra luggage space.

Although the footwells are quite spacious, nothing else about the inside of the car is. Even the simple bench seat has to have the bottom cushion buttoned back in the centre to make enough space for the gear lever in the top gear position.

The level, as befits a motorcycle engined car, is of the quadrant type.

The original Berkeley sports was a pretty looking little car, rather like a scaled down version of the AC Ace, later to become the AC Cobra with fatter tyres, a fatter engine and revised frontal appearance.

The Royal Enfield engined version of the Berkeley also required a lot of revision to its front end appearance to accommodate the bigger engine. Jack admits the result is not particularly handsome, though he says its looks do grow on you.

Overall he says the car is a delight to drive, except in heavy traffic when the driver's field of vision below the glass line of other vehicles becomes limited, and it can still provide the cheap thrills it was built for.

DOUBLE  THINK

(1) Irving at Large

Technically extremely interesting, ultra-sporting in appearance and an almost unknown quantity so far as driving characteristics were concerned. That, up to a month ago, was the new three-wheeler produced by Berkeley Cars, Ltd., of Biggleswade, and powered by the 328 c.c. Excelsior "Talisman Twin" two-stroke. So what more obvious than to try out the prototype in the hands of Phil Irving and Norman Sharpe—our technical authority with no previous three-wheeler experience and our Sports Gossiper, innocent of technical pretensions but with thousands of three-wheeled hours in his log? That is what we did, and here is the result.

AS the front-wheel-drive three-wheeler with trailing third wheel had always seemed to me a very logical layout, it was interesting to have an opportunity to sample the behaviour of the 328 c.c. Berkeley, especially as my previous experience of driving three-wheelers was nil and my experience of front-wheel drive was not much greater.

So far as general handling was concerned, with two people and a modicum of luggage on board, totalling some 20 stone, there seemed to be very little difference in "feel" between the Berkeley and a four-wheeler, except in the interim period between " power-on " and " power-off " conditions when the front end was inclined to wander a little, especially if the surface was at all rough. But there was nothing dangerous about it—merely a sensation that the model had to be held on course instead of running straight of its own accord, as it did either when pulling or during braking.

Naturally most corners were taken in the approved fashion by accelerating round with as much throttle as circumstances permitted, so that the front was, in fact, dragged round by the wheels. However, on one occasion when the ignition switch was accidentally knocked into the " off " position just as a change to third was made before rounding a sharpish right-hander, the unexpected interruption of power did not have any adverse effect.

Many miles of winding, narrow lanes were traversed and the moderate overall width was found to be very helpful when passing slower vehicles; for this exercise third gear, in which 40 m.p.h. was frequently exceeded, came in very handy. On more open roads, 20 miles were covered in 31 minutes, and as there was traffic in plenty and both the route and the car were new to the man at the wheel, the 38 m.p.h. average returned was quite a respectable figure. Fifty m.p.h. was held for much of the time and 60 m.p.h. (by speedometer) attained on the level. Tyre-squeal could be induced round fast open bends, though whether the front or the rear tyres were protesting was a matter of inconclusive conjecture.

Returning to London, partly in dusk and partly in the dark, 65 miles were covered in 2½ hours, though in that time several traffic blocks were met and there were two stops. One was to put up the side curtains to see whether they would make driving conditions a little warmer; since they did not, another stop was made to erect the hood, an operation slightly delayed by the process of discovering which piece went where, although it was really quite a simple matter. The hood effectively eliminated the neck-tickling back-draught from the screen without inducing any of that sense of claustrophobia sometimes experienced under low sports-car hoods, while all-round visibility was good, except upwards.

Considering the small engine capacity the general performance and feeling of liveliness was commendably good—better, one would think, than would be given by a sidecar outfit of equal capacity.

Although the engine would " hang on " down to a few miles per hour if it was forced to do so, full use had to be made of the gearbox on hills or in traffic. Though this component is excellent in itself and almost inaudible in the indirect ratios, the change left much to be desired. This is by means of a lever moving in a notched quadrant and although third-to-top and top-to-third changes could always be made with ease and certainty, that was not the case with the remainder. Neither was it easy to engage bottom from neutral at a standstill—a matter which might be cured by greater backlash between the bottom-gear dogs. With increased familiarity the change would doubtless become easier, but as it stands it is neither so quick as a footchange nor so simple as the hand control of a normal car.

For me, the driving position was ideal, and as my dimensions correspond almost exactly with those of the " average man " postulated by large American car corporations, it would presumably suit most people. The positioning of the pedals, with accelerator and brake at the same level, avoided much of the unnecessary foot movement enforced by the silly layout in some cars. On the other hand there was rather too much leg-room for comfort on the passenger's side.

The high seat-backs gave good support to the shoulders. Though a half-inch or so more padding in the cushions might be acceptable on a long, rough run, the existing amount is adequate for smooth roads and avoids the instability inevitable with deep softly sprung cushions, besides ensuring that the weight is kept low.

Siba starting was certain and silent, both hot and cold, but the noise level of the exhaust when under way was rather too high for pleasurable conversation. Possibly for reasons of efficiency the tail-pipe ends just

abaft of the front wheels; the note, though pleasant in tone, is therefore more audible to the crew than if it emanated from a point farther to the rear. Once or twice the rear suspension bottomed, though this sounded worse than it felt because of a shock-noise generated in the driver's door. The front suspension never bottomed, or at least was never felt or heard to do so.

In the regrettable absence of a gauge, fuel consumption could not easily be checked in stages, but the overall figure for 144 miles of assorted conditions worked out at approximately 67 m.p.g., so no one could complain about running being expensive. Altogether a very pleasant little vehicle which I would have been glad to keep longer.

(2) Sharpe in the Island

THE object of borrowing the Berkeley in the first place was to use it for transport to, at and from the Manx Grand Prix. But only the incredible sturdiness of glass-fibre plastics saved the whole scheme from sabotage the day after I picked the vehicle up from Biggleswade. The driver of a British Railways Scammell on whose nearside I had halted at a wide intersection blithely turned left without a suspicion of a signal and barged the Berkeley in the offside rear. With metal bodywork, that would have meant a lengthy and expensive repair job. As it was it resulted only in an embarrassed B.R. employee, grazed paintwork which was soon cleaned up and a mental note that this three-wheeler's low lines can render it invisible to other drivers in certain circumstances.

Thanks to the Berkeley's phenomenal cornering powers, my two-stage 224-mile journey up to Liverpool took only 5½ hours' driving time, although 60 m.p.h. "on the

clock" was seldom exceeded and the fuel consumption averaged all but 70 m.p.g. Despite Phil Irving's doubts, it was also very comfortable, the divided bench seat giving excellent support and adequately damping the jars caused by occasional bottoming of the rear suspension which was fitted with a lighter spring than will be used on production models. The cockpit noise level was also considerably lower than that of several other three-wheelers I have driven. Also the brakes were unusually powerful—and needed treating with respect.

Several days spent running around Douglas and covering the Two-Days Trial gave ample evidence of the Berkeley's

merits. Fully loaded, no hill could defeat it and one-up there was hardly a gradient it could not surmount in second gear. But the real test was the T.T. Mountain Course. This was no record-breaking effort, for the roads were open and the Island's obligatory Halt signs and 30 m.p.h. speed limits were scrupulously observed. The main object was to see whether we could cover those strenuous 37¾ miles inside the hour, fully loaded.

"Fully loaded" meant with Angus Herbert and myself aboard—a total of some 28 stone. First we were baulked by a bus at Quarter Bridge, but Braddan Bridge was clear and we shot round on the correct side of the centre line with the front wheels gently breaking away as the power came in to tow us up to Union Mills. Down past the "Highlander" the needle flickered over "60," but, knowing the peculiar parking habits of the Manx, I took the blind bend at Glen Helen at about 35—a good 10 m.p.h. slower than I need have done.

The adverse camber just past Appledene had no adverse effect on the Berkeley's handling, though the rough road and the overrun characteristics mentioned by Phil caused it to snake noticeably on the approach to Ballacraine—noticeably but not alarmingly, except perhaps to onlookers. Just before Laurel Bank we collected another bus, but after Creg Willey's—which demanded bottom gear for the steepest stretch—the road was clear again.

Averaging over 50 m.p.h. for the next mile or so, we were well inside our schedule but on the long drop down from Baaregarroo the transmission suddenly tightened and, suspecting an over-warm gearbox mainshaft bearing, I had to ease it off. From then on to Ballaugh we toured at a gentle "45" before stopping to top up the gearbox and refuel with slightly more than half a pint of oil to a gallon of petrol in view of the ensuing Mountain climb.

That started, after two more bus baulks, with a real hash of Ramsey Hairpin. With full lock giving a sort of helical drive, the Berkeley's nose chopped outwards as the left wheel lifted on the corner, losing a lot of way. Even so, we were soon back in

(Left) T.T. stuff. Sharpe applies hard starboard helm to the Berkeley's driven front wheels at Governor's Bridge. Angus Herbert is curiously unperturbed.

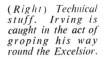

(Right) Technical stuff. Irving is caught in the act of groping his way round the Excelsior.

"second" with the engine screaming its heart out as it hauled us up at 30 m.p.h.

The day was hot and airless and it was too much to expect an air-cooled engine without forced draught to stand that thrashing for long. After several backfires in protest, it ceased to function some way after Guthrie's, though I can't help thinking that it might have made it but for the sheet-metal air scoop. When there is very little draught, this must surely act as a muff which holds the hot air round the cylinders.

When it had cooled off, however, the engine showed no ill-effects and soon took us to the top of the Mountain climb as though nothing had happened. From there, of course, it was all downhill. Taking full advantage of the road, we rounded Windy at about 50 m.p.h. in a gentle drift with bags of room to spare; on the way from Kate's to Creg the needle tickled "70;" and, after chopping round Governor's Bridge, we reached the line again in exactly 62½ minutes' driving time—an average of over 35 m.p.h. Not bad for 328 c.c.!

Further experience showed that the tendency to "snake" on the overrun could be reduced by raising the tyre pressures to about 20 lb. p.s.i. from the 14 inherited from the four-wheeler. Consequently, the only real criticism of this otherwise delightful vehicle concerns its rather harsh clutch and awkward gear change.

Personally, I should also like more power under my right foot. This is not a valid criticism of the vehicle as it is, but it looks and handles so much like a sports car that another 15 or so m.p.h. on the top end would be very welcome, though a higher top gear, already available, would supply a few of these. Certainly other road-users viewing it from in front tended to overestimate its capabilities, often waving it on in circumstances where it had no chance of overtaking. Yet, equally, those who viewed it from behind as "just another three-wheeler" must have been surprised more than somewhat by the way it would run away from them on swervery.

All in all, the Berkeley is a most welcome addition to the three-wheeled ranks, coming close indeed to filling the vacancy in the sports "tricycle" field, which has existed since the demise of the Morgan.

328 c.c. Berkeley Three-wheeler

A Fascinating, Front-wheel-drive Sports Car which Combines Economy with Liveliness and Superb Cornering

By DAVID DIXON

WHEN I first laid eyes on the sleek, aerodynamic styling of the front-wheel-drive Berkeley three-wheeler I immediately classed it as a light sports car with three wheels. Indeed, the car looks almost exactly like its earlier four-wheel counterpart and the constructional details are similar. Body and chassis are formed as a unit. Bonded to the glass-reinforced plastic body are two aluminium-alloy bulkheads and cross-members. The forward bulkhead, with extensions, supports the 328 c.c. twin-cylinder Excelsior two-stroke engine-gear unit and independent wishbone suspension of the front wheels. The other bulkhead provides mounting points for the trailing arm which carries the rear wheel.

Looking at the diminutive size and low build, one might think that space would be cramped. Such is not the case. The 27in-wide doors give easy entry and exit, even with the hood up, and there is ample leg and head room for two large adults.

Settled behind the 16in steering wheel one immediately feels part and parcel of the car. The bench-type seat, which is somewhat thinly padded, is at floor level and consequently one's legs are stretched almost straight to the pendant-type control pedals. For me the seating was just right but the 41in reach from the back of the seat, which is not adjustable, to the pedals might necessitate the use of a back cushion by a person with shorter legs.

Layout of the controls is in orthodox car fashion. I found the accelerator too close to the brake pedal for comfort. The hand brake lever is mounted on the right beneath a capacious parcels shelf. Gear changing is by means of a 7in lever centrally positioned and operating in a gate.

On the standard model which I drove the only instrument on the dashboard was an easily read 120 m.p.h. trip speedometer which proved commendably accurate. Provision is made for mounting a rev-meter, ammeter and fuel gauge, which are all optional extras. The only point about the dashboard layout which called for criticism was the horn button which is to the left of the ignition switch: the button could not be reached easily in a hurry and proved too small for quick operation.

Driving the little Berkeley proved to be a delight. Initially the engine was treated gently as only 215 miles were registered on the milometer. But as the engine and gear box gradually became run-in the pace was increased accordingly. Even at small throttle openings the power available was quite lusty and throughout the throttle range the engine displayed an aptitude for hard work. Acceleration from about one-third throttle opening upward was impressive. Just how lively the vehicle can be was proved by a standing quarter-mile covered (without a passenger) in 26.6s.

Comfortable cruising speed was in the region of 50 m.p.h.

and the mean maximum speed proved to be 60 m.p.h. Thanks to the rubber mountings of the engine, no vibration was felt at any time.

Fuel economy was almost startling. At a steady 30 m.p.h. the consumption was 62½ m.p.g. but at a steady 40 m.p.h. the figure improved to 72 m.p.g. At 50 m.p.h. the consumption averaged 60.8 m.p.g. and the overall figure for the test was just under 60 m.p.g.

Most main-road hills were surmounted in top gear provided a clear run could be obtained. On all but the steepest gradients it was never necessary to drop below third. Starting from a standstill without a passenger on a gradient of 1 in 7 was accomplished with little fuss but with a ten-stone passenger aboard considerable clutch slipping was required. The clutch, incidentally, was fierce in its take-up of the drive.

The gear ratios are very well chosen but a shorter, more precise movement of the lever to give more positive selection would speed up the gear changing. Normal upward changes were made at 14, 25 and 35 m.p.h. but in restricted areas top gear could comfortably be engaged well below 30 m.p.h. Indeed, the Berkeley would woffle along happily at 20 m.p.h. in top gear and the speed could be dropped right down to 12 m.p.h. before transmission snatch set in. If the need arose the speedometer needle could be made to indicate 18, 33 and 44 m.p.h. in the indirect ratios. Full advantage could be taken of the acceleration without offending bystanders, for the exhaust note was excellently subdued.

One of the most endearing characteristics of the Berkeley is its roadholding. No matter what antics I performed there was never any indication that I was driving a three-wheeler. As with most front-wheel-drive cars, power must be applied when cornering as otherwise considerable under-steer results. When cornering quickly over undulations the rear wheel tended to step out a few inches but that merely added to the zest. With the power turned on, sharpish bends could be rounded really fast without the slightest suggestion of the inside wheel lifting. The chosen line could be adhered to within a hair's breadth. The higher the speed, the lighter the steering became. There was virtually no castor action.

Over all normal main roads the comfort afforded by the independent suspension was first class. With a passenger aboard, the rear suspension unit was prone to bottom over fairly rough surfaces. The front suspension could also be made to bottom but only under extreme conditions. In keeping with the general performance, the braking was faultless. The stopping figure achieved was 30ft from 30 m.p.h. The lights allowed full performance to be used at night and, when dipped, gave a satisfactory cut-off.

A surprising feature of the Berkeley is the amount of stowage space. Behind the bench seat is an occasional seat for two small children and behind that there is space enough for several travelling bags or small suitcases. Capacious side pockets provided in the doors are useful for maps and odds and ends. A factor which did *not* impress was the lack of a fuel reserve tap.

What little maintenance would normally be required bearing in mind the two-stroke engine and straightforward construction can be carried out easily with the tool kit provided.

Above: View of the functional cockpit showing the dashboard layout. The knobs on the left control the headlamp and windscreen wipers, next is a blanked orifice for a rev-meter; the second blanked-off space is for an ammeter and fuel gauge. Ignition switch, horn and starter buttons are in the middle. Trafficator switch and warning flasher are on the extreme right. Below: There is ample room in the tail for luggage

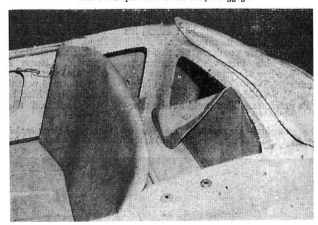

Below: The Excelsior power unit is rubber mounted; drive to the front wheels is through a differential and half-shafts

SPECIFICATION

ENGINE and TRANSMISSION: Air-cooled, petroil-lubricated, Excelsior 328 c.c. (58 x 62mm) twin-cylinder two-stroke in unit with Albion four-speed-and-reverse gear box. Primary drive by chain through a multi-plate wet clutch. Secondary drive by chain to a differential and then through Hardy-Spicer universal joints and half-shafts to the front wheels. Gear ratios: bottom, 25.77 to 1; second, 15.72 to 1; third, 11.09 to 1; top, 7.98 to 1; reverse, 27.53 to 1.

ELECTRICAL EQUIPMENT: Siba Dynastart 12-volt starter-generator. Ignition by twin coils. Wipac 5in double-dipping headlamps. Exide 12-volt 32-amp-hour battery. Flasher direction indicators.

SUSPENSION: Independent on all three wheels; unequal-length wishbones at front and trailing arm at rear; control by Armstrong telescopic spring units incorporating hydraulic damping.

WHEELS and BRAKES: 12in-diameter pressed-steel wheels with five-stud fixing. Michelin 5.20in-section tyres. Girling 7in hydraulic brakes, twin leading shoe front and leading and trailing rear. Cable-operated hand brake on rear.

FUEL CAPACITY: 3½ gallons. Petroil ratio, 16 to 1.

DIMENSIONS: Track, 3ft 9in (overall width, 4ft 2½in); wheelbase, 7ft 3in (overall length, 10ft 4in); weight, with full equipment (including tools and jack) and approximately 1½ gallons of petroil, 763 lb.

PRICE: Basic, £330 11s 4d; including British purchase tax, £399 19s 11d.

MANUFACTURERS: Berkeley Cars Ltd., Hitchin Street, Biggleswade, Beds.

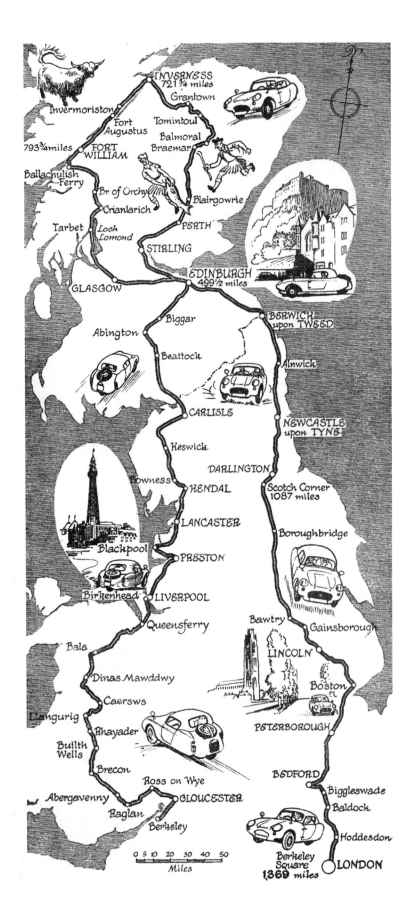

We Went

"WELL all right," said André Baldet, that most dynamic of long-distance trippers, "so we take this Berkeley three-wheeler and we go somewhere and finish in Berkeley Square, yes? Now, where shall we start?" But the answer to that one seemed so obvious. "Well, Berkeley itself," I suggested, "a place down beyond Gloucester. Has a castle. Mentioned in Shakespeare."

"That's it!" enthused André, "Berkeley to Berkeley Square by Berkeley! Bob and Baldet belt around in a Berkeley!" (He always thinks in headlines.) "And tell you what; let's make it a 'B' run, going through places like Blackpool and Boston and . . . what's in Wales?"

We spread out the map. "You could put in Brecon," I commented, "and Builth Wells and Bala. But isn't that a long way round to get to London? Might as well include Braemar while we are at it!" André agreed. He *would*. "Yes," he added, "and then there's that castle place of the Queen's. You know; Balmoral. Then we could cross over and have a look at the six-days' boys at Fort Williams."

"Fort Williams" sounded like something left over from the American frontier days. But so we continued, jotting down the names of places here and there, linking them up into a possible route and then dumping the whole problem into the lap of the A.A. After a particularly slick piece of work in the routes-preparation department, back came a thick wad of strip maps, comprising a total mileage of more than 1,500 miles. As it happened, we didn't manage to do everything we had intended to do. But it was quite a ride, for all that.

First, the three-wheeler. It was a standard hard-top model with 328 c.c. Excelsior Talisman twin two-stroke engine, four-speeds-and-reverse Albion gear box and front-wheel drive. André and I collected the Berkeley from Biggleswade a few days beforehand, and the intention was that it should be nicely run in before the journey began; but Baldet is a busy man, and there was only time to put about 300 miles on the clock, add a spare-wheel

to "Fort Williams" as Well

carrier (a Baldet-designed accessory) and give everything a once-over with the spanners.

On the Sunday, André had been scrambling away for dear life—a real glutton for punishment, this man. A bath, a meal, and he was ready for the first part of the journey down to Gloucestershire. Berkeley certainly has got a castle, a remarkably fine one. And it has also a pub to be proud of in the Berkeley Arms; not many hotels would be prepared to lash out huge plates of bacon and eggs (eggs in the plural) at 5 o'clock in the morning.

This was it; the trip was on. A dull morning, a misty morning, with barely enough light for a start photograph at 6 a.m., but with clear roads André headed the car out on to A38 in the direction of Gloucester. He weighs over 13 stones; so do I. Add in luggage for both, plus a jerrican of petrol, the spare wheel and a portable radio, and the result is quite a load for a little three-wheeler.

We had set ourselves a schedule of 35 m.p.h., which at the outset had seemed optimistic for such a small unit with such a super cargo, but Baldet pressed on regardless, through Gloucester and on up the wooded road to Ross-on-Wye, eating up the miles on the almost deserted roads. In that way, 41.8 miles were packed into the first hour which—with a not-yet-run-in engine—could be classed as pretty good going.

One thing, though; that single rear-suspension unit was a little on the flabby side, with a tendency to bottom on bumpy going, and it was to spell trouble later in the run. But here was the sun, flooding the road to Abergavenny although the hills still lay under a misty shroud and so, to the bright early-morning music of Sid

Down the road from Builth Wells the three-wheeler purrs into Rhayader market place

Upper: Dawn over Gloucestershire. At Berkeley, André studies the route which lies ahead.
Lower: A brief peer at the pier, but no time for rock at Blackpool

Phillips and his band issuing from the portable, we came to the first of our "check-points," B for Brecon.

Builth Wells was right ahead but—which road to take? The valley route through Erwood? Or the bleaker run past Upper Chapel and up over Mynydd Eppynt? We were feeling adventurous, so the mountain road it was, with the car pulling steadily on the gradient and bottom cog required for only a short distance on the rise above Upper Chapel. This was a road I knew, and I wanted to show André the glorious roof of Wales. But it was not to be, for the clouds hung low and soon we were feeling our way through mist.

A squirrel by the roadside stared in wonderment at our passing then scampered off towards the trees and now here was Rhayader, and a rendezvous with photographer Donald Page. We had a few minutes in hand for greetings, a quick cup of coffee and a picture or two before it was time to light out again, towards Llangurig and Caersws. The railway embankment beside the road to Llanidloes, I explained to André, had never carried a train, for the company which built it ran short of cash and never finished the line. Full of scraps of useless information, that's me.

After Cemmaes Road the mountains began to close in; there was some stiff climbing to come and soon, after Dinas Mawddwy, we were tackling the ever-steepening road over the Bwlch Oerddrws pass. Third gear, second, then bottom for the

Up and up and up, over the bare hills of Aberdeenshire climbs the Tomintoul road. Snow pockets line the roadside at the crest. At 1,160 ft, Tomintoul is the highest village in the Highlands

1 in 5 stretch to the summit—and a sudden, ominous screech from the sorely tried engine as the crest was reached. André, at the wheel, jammed his foot down on the clutch pedal. But it was a false alarm—pre-ignition, not a seizure—and the descent to Dolgelley allowed the engine to cool right off.

Along the lakeside at Bala we grew increasingly aware of a rattle from somewhere underneath, and a quick stop revealed that the silencer was chafing against the body; the welding at the front end was giving way. Some time, somehow, we must do something about it, but for the present there was the schedule to maintain, by Ruthin, Mold and Queensferry to Birkenhead, and the Mersey Tunnel. "Is that three wheels or four?" asked the tunnel attendant, "I can't see from here." Nor could I reach him from the passenger's seat with my proffered ninepence. Idea; cut a sliding hatch in the toll booth for the convenience of Berkeley owners!

The Welsh hills had robbed us of much of our initial time advantage, and Liverpool's crowded and bumpy Scotland Road completed the robbery. But a few minutes were snatched back before B for Blackpool came in sight. The town, according to Stanley Holloway's recitation, is "noted for fresh air and fun;" to that we could add "hot pies," for those we bought—and ate while continuing the trip—were really delicious. Wonder if they do a postal service, like the Manx kipper folk?

Here was Kendal at last, and then a switchback run to drop into Bowness, on Windermere. More lakes followed—Rydal Water, Grasmere and Thirlmere—and some grand scenery; but up near Thirlmere they were remaking the road, and when they remake a road in Lakeland they really do make a job of it, even to turning the mattress. We jolted along the hummocks to safe ground at the far side and so, by Keswick, to Carlisle.

"Scotland," said the nameboard at the side of the road. We cheered, said appropriate things like "Hoots, mon!" and "Och, aye!" to each other, and pressed on through the gathering dusk towards Edinburgh, the overnight stop. And it was a damp, grey Edinburgh that greeted us. But we were happy enough, for the little Berkeley had packed 500 miles into a

time of 14 hours and 8 minutes, an average speed of 35.3 m.p.h. so far, including stops for pictures and meals.

Another 6 a.m. start, another damp, grey morning as we took to A9, the road to Perth. But there was a promise of brighter weather ahead. At Kirkliston a plume of steam from a stationary locomotive rose vertically into the still air; there was a gleam in the sky on the horizon. And the first route-marking arrows told us that we were on the way to "Scottish" country—but that was still some way ahead.

Soon there were 50 miles on the clock since leaving Edinburgh, and the average speed was just on 40 m.p.h.; at Bridge of Isla there was time to admire the tall beech hedges ("planted in 1746 and one of the arboreal wonders of the world," the notice board informed us), then on again to Blairgowrie. Here we pulled in to Harper's Garage. The offending silencer was removed, the joint rewelded; the garage chaps worked willingly and well,

but the stop cost us just over an hour.

From the packhorse bridge at Spital of Glenshee onward we were truly for it, with the road climbing upward and upward and the notorious 1 in 5 of the Devil's Elbow to be tackled. But we needn't have worried. The car purred on with never a falter right to the summit, where there were snow pockets on each side of the road. This was 2,199 feet up, the highest classified motor road in Britain (so said our A.A. route card).

Along Royal Deeside, with the river burbling over its rocky bed on the right of the road and pine trees clothing the hills on both sides, the going was as pleasant as any we had yet seen. And with the silencer repaired the chattering from the rear had disappeared. We checked the fuel consumption at Ballater. The overall figure was remaining at 50 m.p.g., the tough road to Braemar notwithstanding.

Tough? We had seen nothing yet! For we were off to the lonely town of Tomintoul, a trip neither of us had made before, and we had little idea of what was in store. But we were soon to learn.

As far as Cock Bridge the run was mild enough, but then I spotted a road, like the side of a house, climbing up the hill to our right. "They *can't* mean us to go up there," exclaimed André, incredulously. But of course they did. And so, with fingers crossed, we set the little car at the gradient, which went up, and up, and up—and when we heaved a sigh of relief at reaching the top we found that the road went up, and up, and up again, in seeming never-ending fashion, to reach the Aberdeen-Banffshire boundary. For sheer fun we had never come across the like before.

But if Tomintoul has a lonely setting, then Granton-on-Spey has a truly lovely one. Aye, a grrrand wee toun. On through Carrbridge, with the main line of the one-time Highland Railway accom-

Fort William offers a breathing space for an hour or two. Bob and André chat with Ken Jones (497 Ariel) at the end of the second day's run in the Scottish Six Days' Trial

panying us to Slochd Summit on the moors above Inverness, and we topped a rise to admire the scene out across the Moray Firth.

So far we had maintained our 35 m.p.h. average from Edinburgh—except for the hour at the garage. There would be no chance whatever of gaining ground on our intended loop northward through Dingwall and across to Ullapool. What should we do?

Well, since the route was of our own choice and we were not out to break records we thought we might cut the course and, instead, follow Loch Ness and the Great Glen down to Fort William. In that way we could stop off for a couple of hours and see a little of the trial. And that was just what we did.

As a souvenir of Fort William, André had bought himself a tartan shirt—and since there was no MacBaldet in stock he settled for Clan Campbell. And me a McDonald, too! As we drove on through rugged Glencoe I told him the story of the massacre; but he wouldn't turn back, to swap the shirt for one of another pattern.

For the night part of the run the average speed schedule was slackened to 30 m.p.h., and on the new timing we reached Bridge of Orchy with a quarter of an hour in hand. Right turn at Crianlarich on to the Glasgow road—but it seemed at first as though we had struck a scrambles course, for road works are in hand and at present the going for the first mile or two of A82 is sheer agony. But it soon eases off, and there followed a pleasant drop through a tree-lined valley to the head of Loch Lomond. Then on again, with the lights of a cottage on the far bank reflected in the still waters, through Tarbet.

But it was raining again in Glasgow, and a wet Glasgow makes a depressing picture. Nor is the signposting all that it could be, and we found ourselves in Coatbridge instead of on the main road to Edinburgh. A diversion at Airdrie brought us back to A8, and with the windscreen wipers swishing to and fro we steamed on down a magnificently graded highway, gaining minutes by the handful.

For the major part of the night run the A1 route through Berwick was on the menu, an oddly deserted A1 in this part of the world. We hoped to run non-stop through the night, but André was feeling drowsy and so we pulled into a convenient lay-by for a half-hour break. With Currie at the wheel we drove out of Newcastle into the dawn, and on through Darlington to Scotch Corner, where we switched back to the 35 m.p.h. schedule. With over a 1,000 miles behind us, the engine was running as sweetly as any sewing machine, and by this time the fuel-consumption figure had improved to 67 m.p.g.

What a honey of an engine the Excelsior is—just the right power unit for a sporting little car such as the Berkeley. On the open A1, which in its northern stretches is now almost up to motorway standard, we seemed to skim over the surface in a completely effortless manner, zizzing the miles away and hugging the road like a racing car.

Off to the left at Bawtry, and through the flat Lincolnshire countryside we made for Boston—familiar going for Baldet,

On the home stretch now, with Baldock already in the bag and Buntingford yet to be collected. Baldet swings the three-wheeler through a Hertfordshire S-bend

who had done his flying training in the area during the war—and there was time to stop for a chat with Stan Cooper, who showed us the power unit of his modified Ariel Arrow for the T.T.

Next Spalding, with the patchwork colours of the tulip fields stretching away to the horizon, then back to the A1 and the turning to Bedford. We were on the home stretch now, and at Biggleswade, where the car was built, a stop was made at the factory to swap the rear-spring unit and the damaged silencer.

The hive of " Bs " was almost full, with just Baldock, Buntingford and Broxbourne to add to the list and then, at last, the run in down Baker Street to an appropriate finish at Berkeley Square. Everywhere, flags were out to greet us; but no, not so, we were told—someone or other was getting married. How were we to know? We hadn't seen a newspaper for days!

Now for the figures. We covered 1,369 miles. Road time including all stops except the overnight stay in Edinburgh and the few hours spent in Fort William, came to 42h 29m, an overall average of 32.2 m.p.h. We collected over 30 Bs. And what did it all prove? Simply that two cylinders, three wheels and two people can add up to a whole lot of enjoyment. And that a Berkeley is a transport of delight, a car with a personality of its own. I wouldn't have missed that trip for worlds.

And so, at last, to Berkeley Square, where the team is greeted on arrival by George Edwards (left) of Berkeley Cars. On the right is Mrs. Baldet

THE BERKELEY

A little giant-killer

BY JOHN F. WOODS

Barely over 10 ft long, the Berkeley was truly the basic sports car. This is the 1957 2-cylinder, 2-stroke, 328-cc Excelsior-powered model. Weather protection was by fabric top, attached after frame was erected.

Berkeley—a name unfamiliar to most car enthusiasts, even dyed-in-the-wool sports car buffs. Few people today have ever heard the name. The automobile's brief production period, only five years, contributed to its obscurity, but obscure or not, it was and still is an interesting marque.

As the British have done before, the Berkeley was ahead of its time. The fiberglass body was a stressed part, the independent suspension on all four wheels kept it glued to the road and the tiny 2- or 3-cylinder motorcycle engine gave sprightly performance with good fuel economy. All in all, it was an attractive, tidy little package. And it *was* little. Compared to the Honda CRX's 145-in. length, the Berkeley's was just 123 in.

The prime movers of the car's production, who represent a link with a fascinating period in automotive history, are still living in England. This is their story:

It all started when Laurie Bond—of the Bond Mini-car and the later Bond Equipe coupes—sought out Charles Panter with plans for a lightweight, front-wheel-drive race car for hillclimbs. Panter was an award-winning designer and a manufacturer of caravans.

In the little hillclimber, however, Panter saw an economical sports car for the European masses and a perfect fill-in product for the slack winter months in the caravan trade. After purchasing the plans from Bond, Panter redesigned the car for road use. It was strengthened, bits and pieces were added to make it legal on the road and the design was revised for mass production.

At the same time the English Anzani Co, which supplied the engine for the historic first flight across the English Channel in 1909, was producing a 2-stroke, 1-cylinder motorcycle engine. Panter and this company collaborated to produce the first Berkeley powerplant. Though incredibly small by American standards, the 2-cylinder 322-cc engine was appropriate for narrow twisty roads, costly gasoline and racing-class displacements of postwar England and Europe. A combination electric starter/generator was added and a small transmission with a reverse gear was adapted. Wheels, differential and other pieces were designed and redesigned to make the car more roadworthy. And only nine months after the purchase of the design, three completed cars stood in front of Panter's Berkeley Coachworks Ltd.

In early September 1956, the British entrepreneur displayed several of his trailers at the Manufacturers and Traders Motor Show in London, a display of mobile homes and house trailers. Because of his fine reputation, he was allowed to show the Berkeleys as an added attraction. And the three cars, virtually handmade, were the hit of the show. The *London Daily Mail* did an article on the runabout, heralding it as the common man's sports car. Within a fortnight, Mr Panter and the Berkeley were mentioned in more than 20 national British newspapers. And in early October the cars were again the hit of another exhibit, the London motor show. The world, especially England, was hungry for transportation that was economical and fun.

Panter set up mass-production facilities for the little phenomenon while under a constant barrage of orders, offers and counteroffers. Problems developed with the Anzani engine and its parent company, so Panter switched to the Excelsior 328-cc 2-cylinder, picking up several horsepower in the bargain.

It was a madhouse of activity. Cars side-by-side on the production line were sometimes different; but each succeeding Berkeley was stronger, more reliable. Another cylinder was added to the Excelsior powerplant, making it 492 cc and producing 30 bhp. This model, the B90, is sometimes called the 500 and is probably the model best remembered in the United States.

Panter made a whirlwind tour of the U.S. and established dealerships. And shortly thereafter a few cars began to arrive in America. Then problems with the fiberglass and its supplier began as some of the bodies developed bubbles after drying, and Panter took legal action.

Meanwhile, Berkeleys began to win everything in their class from hillclimbs to rallies to out-and-out battles with MGs and the like on race courses around England. They often won against cars with engines many times larger.

But at the same time, reports of engine problems began to filter in from the U.S. The 2-cycle that was so at home under the cool skies of the green English countryside wasn't holding up on the long hot freeways of America. At that time—20 years before the wave of Japanese 2-stroke motorcycles—America wasn't all that familiar with 2-stroke engines. Panter received calls and letters asking when to change the oil. Reports came in from dealers about Berkeleys that had been run without oil, the owners not realizing they were supposed to add it to the gas. Cars run flat-out on freeways were then idled in city traffic jams. The effect on the air-cooled engine that didn't have a fan can be imagined. And a problem with the ignition points and the distributor housing cropped up. It was supposed to have been corrected on the new 3-cylinder at the factory by the Excelsior Co; it wasn't. Another lawsuit, another engineering change, another slowdown in getting the car perfected.

But, again, on the other side of the coin, Berkeleys were winning everywhere. In SCCA racing it won the Modified Cars I class in 1958, 1960 and 1961. In 1959 it won the J Production class, its class in the 12-hour enduro at Monza

The 3-cylinder 492-cc Excelsior engine was the basis for Berkeley's competition efforts, which included an almost under-the-table Liège-Brescia-Liège rally run and, of course, extensive circuit racing in England. PHOTO BY KURT WÖRNER

Tested by R&T in 1960, the 692-cc B-95 enjoyed steering input by David E. Davis and navigation by Dean Batchelor. With 40 bhp, it got to 60 mph in 17.2 sec and eventually to its 82.5-mph maximum.

and the Mille Miglia. It outran, outcornered and outhandled everything from MGs to Jaguars. It was a little giant-killer. A 3-wheeler and several experimental wide-bodied Berkeleys were built and marketed in England.

The search for a more conventional, more powerful engine was started as well as a redesign for the front end because of headlight-height regulation in the United States. There also had been murmurs, official and otherwise, about the smoking of the 2-stroke engine. Several engines were tried before a suitable powerplant was found from a company willing to work on the adaptation. The Royal Enfield 2-cylinder, 692-cc 4-stroke motorcycle engine was chosen, and work was started on shoehorning it into a Berkeley.

Then a fire damaged the assembly line and parts-storage area, and the lawsuit with the fiberglass company was lost. The inevitable raising of prices on the new Enfield model plus the new Sprite by Austin-Healey slowed sales.

The Enfield was installed and marketed at the sacrifice of the small sharklike front end. Though blunt-looking the new B95 model again outdistanced all

competition and confounded the mechanics and drivers of the more conventional cars. But the Enfield-engine Berkeley was the company's swan song. Because of the combined losses of the

Last chance to steal modest hearts was the Bandit, which lost the special Berkeley appeal by trying to look too normal. Downright conventional, with 4-cylinder Ford 105E engine, it had no chance against BMC Sprite and Midget.

fire, the lawsuits, warranty work on the cars and the introduction of the Bugeye Sprite, the life of the petite fiberglass wonder came to an end.

In a last-ditch effort, Panter secured the help of John Tojeiro, stylist of the AC Bristol that later became the Ford Cobra, to help design the final Berkeley, the Bandit. This time he used parts that were completely conventional and readily available from the Ford Anglia.

The Bandit turned out to be a clean-looking roadster with a front end reminiscent of a Ferrari and a straightforward rear end with small taillights. It had such interesting features as an independent rear suspension fashioned out of the stock live axle and Girling disc brakes in front, a rarity at that time. The engine was the stock 105E Ford 4-cylinder, 997-cc water-cooled 4-stroke. Like all Berkeleys, it was fiberglass but had a steel floor pan much like the VW Beetle. It was a clean, crisp, conventional design but it was too late. Panter couldn't find financial backing and only two were built (one recently surfaced in London).

So ended a fascinating segment of automotive history. Five short years. The blink of an eye. Approximately 4000 Berkeleys of all configurations were built. They ranged in price from $800 to $2000 and are scattered throughout the world from Santa Barbara to Singapore.

Driving the Berkeley was nothing short of a delight. One didn't so much climb into a Berkeley as *wear* it. You were a part of it and it quickly became a part of you. It was nimble, had a unique sound and produced enough power to delight anyone. The speedometer readings always seemed low. All its idiosyncrasies disappeared when you flicked around a curve on a shining day with the wind in your hair. All your cares fell away as the rpm rose to a howl and you snatched 3rd gear and fed it into a bend—all smiles. ◉